THE JET AGE

This volume is one of a series that traces the adventure and science of aviation, from the earliest manned balloon ascension through the era of jet flight.

THE JET AGE

by Robert J. Serling

AND THE EDITORS OF TIME-LIFE BOOKS

TIME-LIFE BOOKS, ALEXANDRIA, VIRGINIA

Time-Life Books Inc.
is a wholly owned subsidiary of

TIME INCORPORATED

FOUNDER: Henry R. Luce 1898-1967

Editor-in-Chief: Henry Anatole Grunwald
President: J. Richard Munro
Chairman of the Board: Ralph P. Davidson
Executive Vice President: Clifford J. Grum
Chairman, Executive Committee: James R. Shepley
Editorial Director: Ralph Graves
Group Vice President, Books: Joan D. Manley
Vice Chairman: Arthur Temple

TIME-LIFE BOOKS INC.

EDITOR: George Constable
Executive Editor: George Daniels
Director of Design: Louis Klein
Board of Editors: Dale M. Brown, Thomas H. Flaherty Jr.,
William Frankel, Thomas A. Lewis, Martin Mann,
John Paul Porter, Gerry Schremp, Gerald Simons,
Kit van Tulleken
Director of Administration: David L. Harrison
Director of Research: Carolyn L. Sackett
Director of Photography: Dolores Allen Littles

President: Carl G. Jaeger
Executive Vice Presidents: John Steven Maxwell,
David J. Walsh
Vice Presidents: George Artandi, Stephen L. Bair,
Peter G. Barnes, Nicholas Benton, John L. Canova,
Beatrice T. Dobie, James L. Mercer

THE EPIC OF FLIGHT

EDITOR: Dale M. Brown
Senior Editor: Jim Hicks
Designer: Raymond Ripper
Chief Researcher: W. Mark Hamilton

Editorial Staff for *The Jet Age*
Picture Editor: Robin Richman
Text Editor: Lee Hassig
Writers: Laura Longley, Glenn Martin McNatt,
John Manners, Victoria W. Monks
Researchers: Carol Enquist Beall, Gregory A. McGruder
(principals), Barbara Brownell, Anne Munoz-Furlong,
Dominick A. Pisano, Jules Taylor
Assistant Designer: Anne K. DuVivier
Copy Coordinators: Stephen G. Hyslop, Anthony K. Pordes
Picture Coordinator: Betsy Donahue
Editorial Assistant: Caroline A. Boubin

Special Contributor: Lynne Bair

Editorial Operations
Production Director: Feliciano Madrid
Assistant: Peter A. Inchauteguiz
Copy Processing: Gordon E. Buck
Quality Control Director: Robert L. Young
Assistant: James J. Cox
Associates: Daniel J. McSweeney, Michael G. Wight
Art Coordinator: Anne B. Landry
Copy Room Director: Susan Galloway Goldberg
Assistants: Celia Beattie, Ricki Tarlow

Correspondents: Elisabeth Kraemer (Bonn); Margot
Hapgood, Dorothy Bacon (London); Susan Jonas, Lucy T.
Voulgaris (New York); Maria Vincenza Aloisi, Josephine du
Brusle (Paris); Ann Natanson (Rome). Valuable assistance
was also provided by: Judy Aspinall (London); Cheryl
Crooks (Los Angeles); Felix Rosenthal (Moscow);
Judy Greene, Christina Lieberman (New York);
Mimi Murphy (Rome).

THE AUTHOR

Robert J. Serling's career as an aviation writer began when he edited aviation news for United Press International, and it evolved into full-time book writing. He has written numerous works of fiction and nonfiction about aviation in the jet age, including *Loud and Clear, The Probable Cause, The Electra Story, The President's Plane is Missing* and the histories of four airlines—Eastern, Western, Continental and North Central.

THE CONSULTANTS for The Jet Age

Richard K. Smith, the principal consultant, is a former historian at the National Air and Space Museum in Washington, D.C. He is the author of several aeronautical histories, including *First Cross! The U.S. Navy's Transatlantic Flight of 1919,* which was awarded the 1972 history prize of the American Institute of Aeronautics and Astronautics. He also serves as American literary editor of the British aviation monthly *Air International.*

R. E. G. Davies, a noted aviation historian, has worked for British European Airways, Bristol Aircraft, the de Havilland Aircraft Company and Douglas Aircraft. The author of *A History of the World's Airlines* and *Airlines of the United States Since 1914,* he is a Fellow of the Royal Aeronautical Society and served in 1982 as the Lindbergh Professor of Aerospace History at the National Air and Space Museum.

For information about any Time-Life book, please write:
Reader Information
Time-Life Books
541 North Fairbanks Court
Chicago, Illinois 60611

Library of Congress Cataloguing in Publication Data
Serling, Robert J.
   The jet age.
   (The Epic of flight)
   Bibliography: p.
   Includes index.
   1. Aeronautics, Commercial—History. 2. Jet transports—
History. I. Time-Life Books. II. Title. III. Series.
TL552.S47 1982   387.7'42'09   82-6019
ISBN 0-8094-3362-1   AACR2
ISBN 0-8094-3363-X (lib. bdg.)

CONTENTS

Precursors of the jets

"Spend a Two-Week Vacation Abroad? Why Not?" asked a Pan American advertisement in 1946, trumpeting both the end of wartime travel restrictions and the beginning of a new day in commercial aviation. Eager to reclaim their prewar markets and expand them, the airlines put into service the largest, most luxurious piston-engined planes ever designed.

In the United States, the development of transports had surged ahead during the War. Douglas, Boeing and Lockheed all had long-range airliners with pressurized cabins on the production line within a year of V-J Day. And it was these planes, with their vastly increased capabilities, that the airlines flocked to buy.

Expecting a postwar boom in domestic and international travel among the well-to-do, the big carriers courted the same first-class trade upon which they had based their business in the 1930s. Seven-course meals, champagne and gifts of orchids and perfume were amenities calculated to distract travelers from the inevitable noise and vibration of the propeller-driven planes, especially on 10- to 12-hour transatlantic crossings. And one-class seating on many flights encouraged socializing in the lounges and dining areas, giving the aircraft the ambiance of elegant ocean liners. Some of the planes even boasted sleeping berths.

But the high fares such lavishness required excluded middle-class travelers; by 1950 most of the airlines were struggling to fill seats on their first-class flights. The future lay in low fares, high-density seating—and ever more speed. Already in the air, as the days of wine and roses aboard the piston airplanes ended, were the prototypes of the jet airliners that would change the character and spirit of air transportation forever.

Four generations of propeller-driven Douglas airliners sit on the ramp at the factory in Santa Monica, California. In the background is a prewar unpressurized DC-3. Immediately in front of it are a four-engined DC-4 and a DC-6. And in the foreground is a DC-7, last of the line before the arrival of jet transport and a new age of flight.

The DC-6: the "ultimate in travel relaxation"

The DC-6 Dayplane-Sleeper could berth 26
passengers or seat 52. Promoted as the
"ultimate in travel relaxation," it contained
lounges fore and aft of the cabin, and
a buffet area in the middle of the plane.

A flight attendant tucks in a blanket on the upper berth while a passenger retires below. Such berths, made up before takeoff, took just 30 seconds to ready. Both sleeper and daytime accommodations could be used at the same time in some versions of the DC-6.

A young model who would go on to fame as Marilyn Monroe relinquishes her coat to a Pan American flight attendant to store in a cloakroom. Overhead racks would not appear until the onset of the jet age during the next decade.

The Stratocruiser: offspring of the War

A double-decked Boeing 377 Stratocruiser wings over Rio de Janeiro. Cruising at 340 mph, the 70-ton plane, a descendant of the B-29 bomber of World War II fame, was the biggest and fastest airliner flying in 1948.

Carrying only 61 passengers in 6,600 cubic feet of "ambling space," the Stratocruiser boasted a forward family travel compartment and a lounge on the lower level below the midship galley.

A passenger adjusts his tie in the men's dressing room. Flying at 25,000 feet avoided most turbulence and allowed passengers to move about the plane safely.

A steward serves wine to a couple eating dinner. The tray-tables, designed by Boeing, were the first to attach to seats.

Passengers relax in the lower-level lounge. Reached by a spiral staircase, the softly lit compartment was decorated with rich fabrics and leather to suggest a fine club.

The Constellation: an ocean-hopping beauty

Put into service in 1957, the triple-tailed Lockheed 1649A Constellation brought every West European capital within nonstop reach of New York. It carried 56 passengers.

A flight attendant offers coffee to a card-playing couple. The spacious lounge featured colorful murals and an observation sofa facing a starboard window.

Passengers board a TWA night flight to Europe. TWA received its first Connies in April 1957 but had them in service for only 18 months before rival Pan Am inaugurated jet flights over the North Atlantic.

A European diversity

The de Havilland Airspeed Ambassador, powered by two Bristol Centaurus engines, was British European Airways' standard short-haul airliner from 1952 to 1958. The plane's 550-mile range made it ideal for BEA's routes on the Continent.

Passengers enjoy a meal aboard the Ambassador's luxury Silver Wing service. The high ceiling of the cabin was popular for the extra roominess it provided.

The double-decked Brequet 763 Deux-Ponts, a French military transport adapted to civilian use in 1953, was one of the first airliners fitted out for mass travel. Though only one third larger than an American DC-6, the craft carried almost twice the number of passengers: 59 in tourist class on its upper deck and 48 in second class on its lower deck; there was no first class.

Cars are loaded through a rear door in the lower deck of the Deux-Ponts. To convert the deck, the hinged passenger seats were folded flat against the cabin walls.

Stillborn giants

Taking off with the aid of rockets, a 92-ton Lockheed Constitution struggles aloft in 1946. Underpowered in spite of four 3,500-hp engines, the plane failed to reach its proposed 5,000-mile range and never went into commercial service.

The only Bristol Brabazon ever built stands outside the hangar at Filton, England. Weighing 145 tons, the eight-engined craft carried only 80 passengers. Before the Brabazon could fly, the runway had to be extended, houses razed and a road diverted.

A Convair XC-99, able to carry 400 passengers, makes its debut in San Diego in 1947. Powered by six pusher engines, this descendant of the massive B-36 bomber was intended as a troop transport and cost $15 million to develop. Only one was built.

Hurtling into the sky with a power almost five times greater than that of a piston-engined DC-6, the de Havilland Comet, the first jetliner, leaves London

Airport on its maiden flight to Johannesburg.

1
A leap into the future

A large crowd had gathered at London Airport on the sunny afternoon of May 2, 1952. It had come to see a most unusual aircraft, one bearing the official designation G-ALYP. In the British lexicon of aircraft registration, G-ALYP—called, in the phonetic alphabet, George-Able Love Yoke Peter—stood for a new commercial transport known as the de Havilland Comet.

To most in the crowd, Yoke Peter presented a strange sight: an airplane with no visible means of propulsion, one that seemed to confound logic with its absence of familiar propellers and protruding engine nacelles. The Comet's four engines were buried in the wings, two on each side of the gleaming 93-foot-long fuselage that bore the blue and white livery of the British Overseas Airways Corporation.

There were cheers as Yoke Peter wheeled away from its boarding area, its engines howling. Yoke Peter was the world's first jet airliner, capable of flying at nearly 500 miles an hour, more than half again as fast as its piston-engined contemporaries. It was about to take off for Johannesburg, South Africa, via Rome, Beirut, Khartoum, Entebbe and Livingstone. The journey normally took 40 hours. But the Comet, with its 36 passengers and crew of six, would get there in an unheard-of 23½ hours. In the environment of flight, where distance is measured not by miles but by time, the Comet was about to shrink the globe by 40 per cent—and render every other commercial transport obsolete. But unhappily for this magnificent product of British skill and ingenuity, its name would all too soon be associated with failure and disaster.

In 1952, the airplane had yet to supplant either the train or the ship as a major mode of travel. But it was making inroads on them. In the few years since the end of the War, four-engined American planes—primarily Douglas Aircraft's DC-4s, DC-6s and DC-7s, and Lockheed's graceful, three-tailed Constellations—had replaced the slower flying boats and twin-engined planes as the flagships of the world's major airlines. Attracted by the benefits of speed, more and more travelers were now choosing planes over trains. Before the end of the 1950s, the number of passengers carried by domestic U.S. airlines would exceed the number that boarded the nation's railroads, and international airliners would supplant ocean liners as the most popular way to cross the Atlantic.

But even the best of these aircraft was limited. The Douglas DC-7C, the plane that inaugurated regular nonstop transatlantic service in 1956,

The world's first fare-paying jet travelers— including a man who had booked two years in advance so that he could be called jet passenger No. 1—board the Comet at London Airport for its inaugural flight.

was little more than a 15-year-old design that had been pulled and stretched to carry more passengers plus enough fuel for the jump across the ocean. And the four engines necessary to accomplish this feat were behemoths that produced 3,400 horsepower each; with all 72 cylinders firing on cue, noise and vibration inside the cabin were numbing. More-over, the DC-7C, though it was larger than earlier models and had a greater range, actually flew more slowly. More powerful piston engines were impractical. Existing ones were already a mechanic's nightmare; balky engines all too often were responsible for delaying flights. Com-mercial aircraft had reached a plateau.

Then along came the Comet. Within a decade after Yoke Peter's flight to Johannesburg, travel by jet would be commonplace. And air-lines—at least during the first giddy years of the jet revolution that the Comet started—would be carrying more passengers at lower fares than anyone had dreamed possible. Faraway places, once the haunts of the rich, would become the playgrounds of everyman, transported in a few hours by airliners that could seat more than 400 passengers. For the elite, and for businessmen in an exceptional hurry, the flight from New York to London or Paris would ultimately be slashed to a mere three and a half hours, by a plane that could fly faster than the speed of sound.

The gestation of the Comet dated from 1943, when the British, though still at war, became concerned about their postwar role in commercial aviation. During the War they had dedicated all of their aircraft assembly lines to the production of fighters and bombers, and ceded the transport field to the Americans. In doing so, they realized, they were allowing their ally a tremendous lead. By 1939, Douglas' ubiquitous DC-3 was already carrying 90 per cent of the world's airline passengers. And in the half-dozen years that followed, the Americans managed to perfect two other transports, ideally suited to postwar use as airliners—the four-engined Douglas DC-4 and Lockheed Constellation. The British might never catch up.

This gloomy outlook came under the scrutiny of two successive government study groups, both headed by "the father of British aviation," Lord Brabazon of Tara, and composed of airline executives, manufacturers' representatives and civil service aviation experts. The first Brabazon Committee convened in 1942 and accomplished little. A year later, however, a second Brabazon Committee was organized and over a 30-month period came up with four proposals to move Britain into the transport field. Two of them envisioned huge, piston-engined airliners with luxurious accommodations for transoceanic travelers; both designs turned out to be impractical. Two others argued for airliners powered by jet engines. In one, the engine would be used to turn a propeller. Called a turboprop, such an engine would come to play an important role in commercial aviation, first as the power plant for the Vickers Viscount from Britain and later for America's Lockheed Electra *(pages 25-27)*. Passengers came to like planes with turboprops; they were much quieter than piston-engined aircraft, and airlines found them economical and easier to maintain.

But because of the inherent limitations of propellers, which could be made only so big before becoming inefficient, turboprops were unable to fly much faster than piston craft, and that is why the last of the Brabazon Committee's proposals was intriguing. The idea was to build a transport the size of a DC-3, driven not by propellers at all but by exhaust gases from turbojet engines that would whisk it along at 450 miles per hour. Known at the start only as the Brabazon IV, this concept fathered the Comet and marked a new era in air travel—the jet age.

But in 1945, any jet-powered transport—particularly the Brabazon IV—seemed more dream than practicality. Up to that time, the jet engine had propelled only fighter aircraft, and its prodigious thirst for fuel, in the opinion of many aviation authorities, made it economically unsuitable for commercial aircraft. But for the British the jet's apparent impracticality was more than balanced by one important fact: Jet propulsion was the one branch of aeronautics in which Britain was ahead of the United States—and by a wide margin.

Britain's lead was largely the achievement of one man, an RAF officer named Frank Whittle. As early as 1929 he had proposed that a gas turbine engine be used to power a plane; instead of applying most of the engine's power to a propeller, the turbine would force the exhaust gas out of a rear nozzle with tremendous force—enough to thrust an aircraft forward. Whittle was later to describe this turbojet as "something like a giant vacuum cleaner; it sucks air at the front and blows it out at the back."

It was not quite that simple, of course. More than seven years would go by before a working model of his invention would appear, and another four years before Britain's first jet fighter, the Gloster Meteor, took to the air. But this was more than the United States could manage during that time.

Though several British manufacturers had gained experience making jet engines, there was only one firm at the end of the War that had both built a jet engine and designed a jet plane. The plane was the Vampire fighter, and the company was de Havilland. The respected aircraft manufacturer was the logical candidate for transforming into reality the Brabazon Committee's proposal for a jet-engined transport, and in 1947 the Ministry of Supply asked de Havilland to get on with the work.

Sir Geoffrey de Havilland, the tall, dignified founder of the firm, exuded an enthusiasm for the project that set him apart from his peers in the aviation world. He seemed undaunted by the many problems that would have to be solved before the jet could become reality. The biggest of these was the jet engines' extravagant fuel consumption. In the United States, C. R. Smith, president of American Airlines, had predicted bleakly that to achieve transcontinental or transatlantic range, a jetliner would have to carry so much fuel that there would be little room for a payload. There were those in Great Britain who agreed, pointing out that a turbojet's fuel consumption was at least three times that of a piston engine.

Like any other internal combustion engine, a turbojet will not operate without just the right mix of air and fuel. The limited supply of oxygen many thousand feet above the earth thus makes it impossible for the jet to burn as much fuel as it consumes at lower altitudes, where oxygen is more plentiful. Engines of 1945 vintage, for example, gulped kerosene three or four times as fast at 10,000 feet as they did at 30,000 feet.

Sir Geoffrey recognized that the solution to the fuel problem would be a plane that could operate at altitudes of 35,000 feet and higher. The engines might produce less power at such heights, but—and here was the key—less power would be required to propel the aircraft through thin air. He asked Ronald Bishop, de Havilland's chief designer, and Frank Halford, the company's expert on jet engines, to give him such a plane. Initially, it was known as the D.H.106, but it was renamed the Comet for the Comet Racer, a plane built two decades earlier by de Havilland that had won the MacRobertson Air Race from England to Australia.

Uppermost in the minds of the entire Comet team was the knowledge that the high-flying plane would require an airtight cabin that could be

The ABCs of jet propulsion

The planes that revolutionized air travel in the 1950s resulted from the development of power plants that dispensed with the pounding pistons and intermittent, contained explosions of the conventional engine, using instead spinning turbines and a steady burning of fuel.

With no bulky engine blocks and no pistons, valves or rods to restrict their rpms, the new engines produced far more power for far less weight than piston engines. But they needed inordinate quantities of fuel to generate that power.

The turbojet, the first of three basic engines to evolve, is both the fastest and the thirstiest; it can be used efficiently only at high altitudes, where thin air decreases fuel use and drag. The other two, the turboprop and the turbofan, are adaptations of the turbojet that operate with greater efficiency at lower altitudes and moderate speeds.

All three types have essentially the same core: At the front, whirling fans called compressors suck air in and force it under high pressure into a combustion chamber where it mixes with a steady stream of fuel and is ignited. The expanding gases funnel out the back of the combustion chamber at tremendous speed in a narrow exhaust jet that provides forward thrust. Before the exhaust leaves the engine, however, it passes one or more vaned disks called turbines that the fast-moving gases spin. These turbines, in turn, drive the compressors. In the turboprop and turbofan engines, additional turbines crank a propeller or a fan at the front that creates most of the engine's thrust.

A TURBOJET is essentially a tube that burns a steady stream of compressed air and fuel, blasting exhaust out the back to propel the plane forward. A turbine spun by the exhaust drives the compressors by means of a rotating shaft running down the middle of the engine.

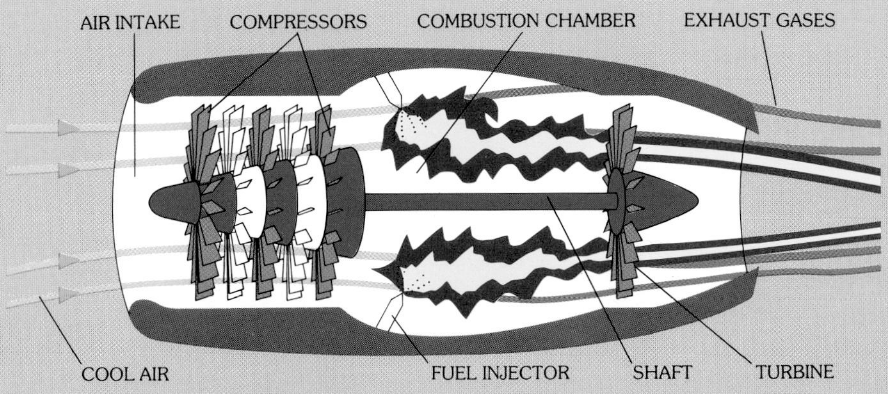

AIR INTAKE   COMPRESSORS   COMBUSTION CHAMBER   EXHAUST GASES

COOL AIR   FUEL INJECTOR   SHAFT   TURBINE

A TURBOPROP uses additional turbines to make the jet exhaust crank a propeller that provides thrust. The rapid spinning of the turbines and their shaft must be geared down to run the propeller at a usable speed.

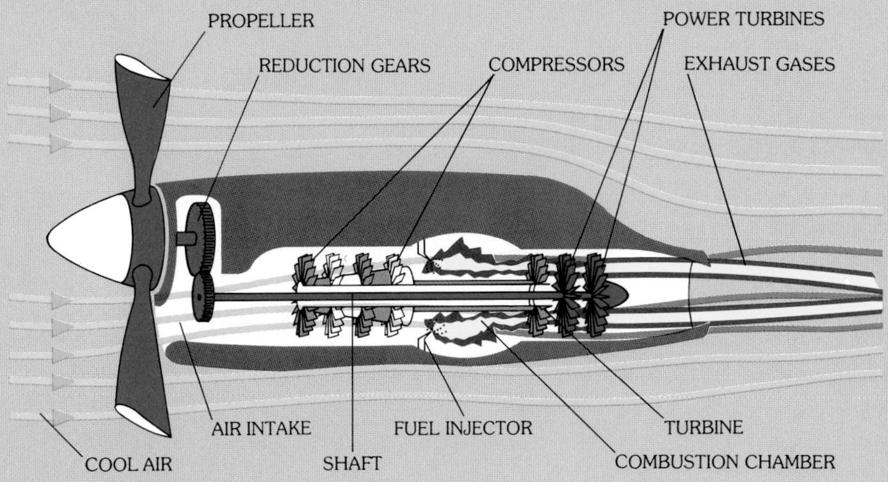

PROPELLER   POWER TURBINES

REDUCTION GEARS   COMPRESSORS   EXHAUST GASES

AIR INTAKE   FUEL INJECTOR   TURBINE

COOL AIR   SHAFT   COMBUSTION CHAMBER

A TURBOFAN'S big fan works much like a turboprop's propeller but also helps to compress air passing through the engine. Most thrust, however, comes from air bypassing the core. This cool, relatively slow-moving air, channeled by the fan's shrouding, forms a surrounding buffer for the rapidly moving, noisy core exhaust and reduces engine noise.

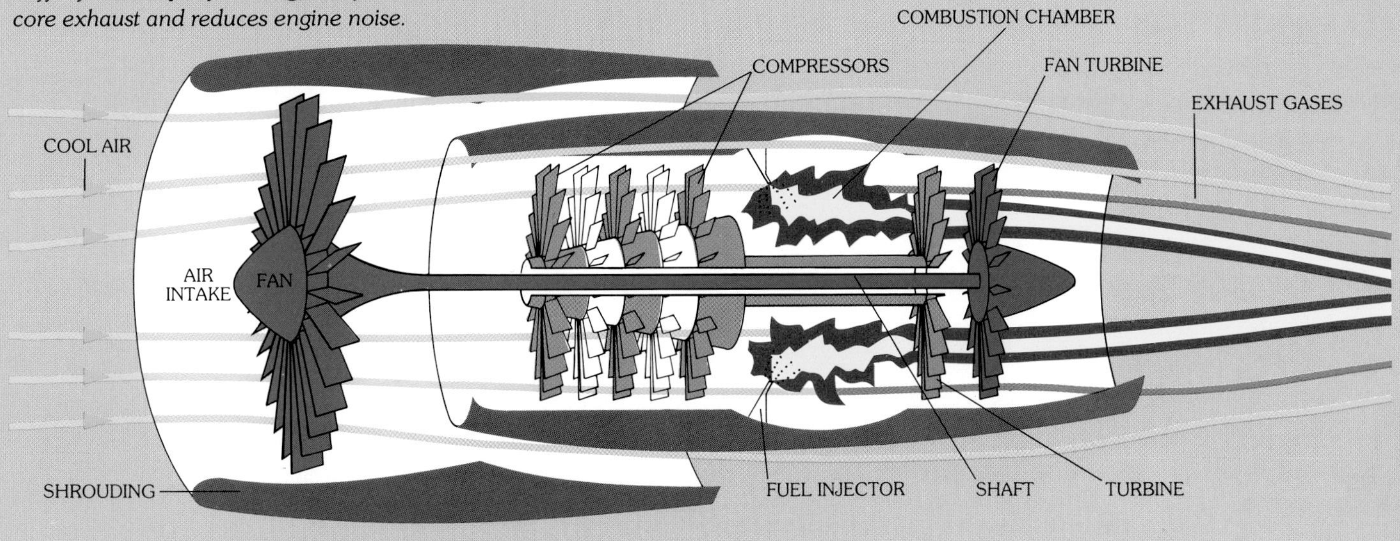

COMBUSTION CHAMBER

COMPRESSORS   FAN TURBINE

EXHAUST GASES

COOL AIR

AIR INTAKE   FAN

SHROUDING   FUEL INJECTOR   SHAFT   TURBINE

pumped full of air under pressure to allow passengers to breathe without aid of oxygen masks. Pressurized aircraft cabins were hardly new. But the Comet, flying above 35,000 feet, would face stresses no other airliner had yet encountered. In order to maintain an atmosphere roughly equivalent to that at 8,000 feet, the pressure inside the cabin would reach eight and a quarter pounds per square inch—some five pounds more than the pressure outside.

Bishop's team of airframe engineers began churning out designs. Of the dozen or so configurations that were considered seriously, the most promising was for a four-engined, tailless craft with elevators and ailerons built into wings swept back 40 degrees. This arrowhead shape was calculated to extract the most speed possible from each pound of thrust.

Before committing himself to so radical a design, Bishop had the idea tested. He had the standard wings and tails of three de Havilland Vampire fighters replaced with triangular wings, each with a different angle of sweepback. But flight tests disclosed serious control problems. As a result, Bishop abandoned a tailless plane in favor of a more conservative design; at a small sacrifice in speed, wings would be swept back only 20 degrees.

The Comet's external appearance and its vital statistics were fairly well fixed by early 1947. The airframe would be as light as de Havilland knew how to make it. The aluminum skin, for example, would be only $28/_{1,000}$ of an inch thick—"no thicker than a postcard," marveled one British writer—and it would be fastened to the plane's skeleton with a special glue called Redux, thus eliminating rivets and making the plane still lighter. Four de Havilland Ghost turbojets would propel the Comet and its three dozen passengers at nearly 500 miles per hour.

Satisfied with the de Havilland engineers' estimate of the Comet's performance, BOAC ordered eight of the airliners and reserved first refusal on any built after the first 14 came off the assembly line. Sales were contingent, of course, on the jetliner's meeting all British civil airworthiness requirements.

No one at de Havilland doubted that the Comet would do so. From the cutting of the first metal to the final certification flights, it would be the most stringently tested British airplane to date. Regulations demanded, for example, that the Comet's cabin hold 16½ pounds per square inch of air pressure, double the actual pressure that would be allowed in the fuselage at the aircraft's maximum cruising altitude. But Bishop's chief structural engineer, Robert Harper, insisted on an extra margin of safety; he designed the Comet fuselage to withstand an internal pressure of more than 20 pounds per square inch. The wings passed a torture test in which the tips were repeatedly raised and depressed three feet from their normal positions. The landing gear was extended and retracted thousands of times—with sand mixed in the grease that lubricated it, to simulate the worst possible conditions.

During the many months required to complete the batteries of tests, de Havilland was silent about its new project. At one point Sir Geoffrey

A British Vickers Viscount 745, one of 60 sold to Capital, a now-defunct U.S. airline, could fly 48 passengers 1,500 miles at 350 mph.

The only U.S. turboprop ever in regular commercial service, the Lockheed Electra carried more than 80 passengers at better than 400 mph but soon lost out to faster jets.

The turboprop: a versatile hybrid

Just over a year before the Comet's initial test flight, the prototype of another revolutionary aircraft became the first jet-powered airliner to fly. The plane, the British Vickers Viscount, was not, however, what is sometimes referred to as a pure jet. It was a turboprop, using propellers powered by the turbines of jet engines *(pages 22-23).*

Though not as fast as a turbojet, the Viscount had other advantages. For one thing, it was far more fuel efficient at low altitudes and moderate speeds, and thus more useful on short flights. For another, it could take off and land on short run-

ways like a conventional piston-engined plane. Moreover, its vastly greater power enabled it to carry larger loads at higher speeds than comparable conventionally powered aircraft.

The Viscount went into commercial service early in 1953 and became one of the most widely used of all short-haul planes. Other turboprops, including the Lockheed Electra *(above)* and the aircraft shown on the succeeding pages, soon followed. A few of them are still serving as commuter airliners or transports wherever distances are relatively short, traffic light and runways limited.

The Russian Tupolev 114, a converted bomber design, used 12,000-hp turboprop engines to turn pairs of 18-foot contrarotating propellers.

In production longer than practically any other commercial transport, the 50-passenger Fokker F-27 became Europe's largest-selling airliner.

De Havilland Canada's 20-passenger Twin Otter, with its sturdy fixed undercarriage, was designed for use on primitive airfields in the bush.

The de Havilland Dash-7, produced in Canada, made medium-sized airliner service possible for airports with runways as short as 2,000 feet.

felt obliged to react publicly to rumors about the aircraft's shape, speed and cruising altitude. The reports, he said, "have been based on conjecture, and whilst they are not without a glimmer of truth here and there, the general effect of categoric statements at so early a stage in the project is inevitably misleading."

Sir Geoffrey's caution was not without purpose. He had no intention of disclosing valuable information to potential competitors, particularly manufacturers in the United States, before the Comet had even flown. Nor did he care to publicize the false starts, wrong turns and divergent views inherent in the creation of a new plane. (For example, both BOAC and British South American Airways, which had placed orders for six Comets, preferred more powerful Rolls-Royce turbojet engines to the de Havilland-designed Ghosts. Eventually the two airlines agreed to accept the first 14 Comets with Ghost engines, provided that the next model, to be called the Comet 2, was powered by Rolls-Royce engines.)

Comet test flights began July 27, 1949, less than three years after the start of full-scale design work. This was no mean feat for a company that, until only five years earlier, had been single-mindedly building warplanes. Sir Geoffrey was on hand to witness the first flight, as were many of those who had labored so diligently to bring the airplane to life. Among the outsiders present was Sir Frank Whittle, who had recently been knighted by King George VI for inventing the turbojet.

In charge of evaluating the Comet—and first to fly it—was de Havilland's chief test pilot, John Cunningham. Accompanied by a crew of engineers to monitor the aircraft's performance, Cunningham eased the jet's throttles forward, and the Comet took effortlessly to the air. Whittle, who had been ill, declared that the sight of the silver plane streaking over the airfield was better than any medicine. Cunningham, after a half-hour flight that took the Comet to 10,000 feet, pronounced the jet "Very promising. Very quick."

And so it was. Over the next three years, as de Havilland's new jet was fine-tuned for airline service, the entire globe became Comet-conscious, and the airlines beat a path to the de Havilland door. Air France, British Commonwealth Pacific, France's Union Aéromaritime de Transport, Canadian Pacific, Japan Air Lines and the Royal Canadian Air Force were among the Comet's first purchasers.

Sir Miles Thomas, BOAC's enthusiastic chief, told a New York audience that eventually the Comets would be flying to America's East Coast and beyond. When that happened, he predicted hyperbolically, "New Yorkers will be able to take a swim in Bermuda and dry themselves at home." But only one U.S. airline joined the jet parade. Some five months after Yoke Peter's first flight to Johannesburg, Juan Trippe, chairman of Pan American World Airways, ordered three Comet 3s, a more powerful version of the plane that was still on the drawing boards. Trippe, as usual infatuated with any airplane that represented a major technological advance, ordered the Comets because there was no U.S.-

Putting the Comet to the test

A jet engine is mounted behind the nose section of a Comet to help technicians determine noise levels inside the cockpit.

Months before finalizing designs for the Comet jetliner in 1946, the de Havilland Aircraft Company undertook an exhaustive testing program of all the jet's components and assemblies.

The most critical of these involved the Comet's structure. To determine how well the wings would stand up to the stresses of flight, they were secured in a huge rig and flexed beyond their design limits. But when it came to proving out the fuselage, de Havilland decided that static testing—subjecting the plane to pressure alone, without motion—would be adequate.

De Havilland constructed a decompression chamber and placed the fuselage in it, then manipulated pressures inside and outside the cabin to simulate conditions the Comet would experience in cold, rarefied air at 38,000 feet. The nose section was brought to nine pounds of pressure per square inch—almost a pound more than the normal Comet in-service pressure would be—and the procedure was repeated 2,000 times. Other fuselage sections were subjected to almost double that amount—16.5 pounds per square inch.

The results of these stress tests were just what de Havilland designers and engineers had hoped for: The Comet held up beautifully, convincing them that they had built the safest jet imaginable.

A wooden mock-up of the Comet is used to experiment with design changes.

A Comet nose is grafted to a Horsa glider fuselage for windshield tests.

Sir Geoffrey de Havilland operates the nose-wheel steering mechanism.

The first Comet fuselage is rolled toward a steel test rig where wings will be attached and forced up and down thousands of times.

Three years after work on the Comet began, the plane completes its first flight, a handling trial that the test pilot declared "entirely successful."

made jetliner on even a distant horizon. To goad American plane builders into the game, Trippe kept on his desk a draped model of the Comet. Whenever a factory representative visited, he whisked off the cover, revealing the British competition.

Trippe's contract with de Havilland stipulated that the Comet 3 must satisfy American safety regulations before Pan American would accept delivery. There was in fact some likelihood that the Civil Aeronautics Administration would not grant the Comet an airworthiness certificate. The CAA had already expressed reservations about the square corners of the aircraft's windows, where stresses could build, leading to metal fatigue, and recommended oval windows instead. The location of the Comet's engines, in the wings close to the cabin, also troubled the CAA. If an engine were to disintegrate in flight, it would be more likely to destroy the plane than an engine hung below the wing, away from the fuselage.

The de Havilland Company felt confident that it could assuage the CAA's doubts. Pressurization tests on the Comet fuselage had clearly demonstrated the strength of the square window frame; one had withstood a pressure of 100 pounds per square inch, more than a 12-fold margin of safety. As for engine failure, turbojets—because of their smooth operation—would enjoy a long and trouble-free life. Moreover, placing the Comet's turbojets in the wings was sound aerodynamics. The wing would be more streamlined, and having the Comet's engines near the fuselage would make the plane easier to handle if an engine were to fail on takeoff. In any event, there was time for de Havilland to modify the Comet to the CAA's satisfaction; Trippe's order would not be filled until 1956, four years after BOAC's first commercial flight.

In service with BOAC, the Comet was an immediate hit. In the initial year of operations, the sleek jetliners carried almost 28,000 passengers a total of 104.6 million miles. Even the Royal Family put its stamp of approval on the jet; the next year the Queen Mother and Princess Margaret flew in a Comet from London to Rhodesia.

By May 1953, de Havilland had on hand firm orders for 50 Comets and negotiations were in progress for another 100. And BOAC, which had estimated that it would have to fill 72 per cent of the seats on each Comet flight to break even, found that in the first 12 months, Comets averaged 88 per cent of capacity. The Comet seemed an unqualified success.

But there was cause for concern, too: The Comet had three serious accidents that year. The first two occurred on takeoff; in both cases, the jetliners simply failed to become airborne. Miraculously, no one died in the first crash, which was blamed on the pilot. But the second accident left no survivors. After the first mishap, investigators took a sharp look at the Comet's takeoff procedures and recommended that pilots attain a higher air speed before pointing the plane's nose skyward. After the second crash, they analyzed

Tense before the first test flight of the Comet prototype, on July 27, 1949, Sir Geoffrey de Havilland (in fedora), Ronald Bishop (center), the Comet's designer, and an unidentified executive wait for the aircraft's takeoff. Sir Geoffrey had gambled four million pounds—$16 million—on the jet's development.

the wing and prescribed a modification that would add lift at low speeds.

The third Comet accident, which occurred on the first anniversary of BOAC's historic inaugural flight to Johannesburg, was a different matter altogether: A Comet plunged into a violent thunderstorm six minutes after taking off from Calcutta and disintegrated in mid-air.

With the causes of the accidents presumably understood, neither de Havilland, the airlines nor British aviation authorities were worried about the Comet's future. To be sure, two of the crashes had unmasked in the jet a peculiar vulnerability on takeoff. But there was never a new transport built that did not develop unsuspected bugs—and this problem had been corrected promptly. The Calcutta crash was written off as no more than a freak accident; turbulent air within a severe thunderstorm can tear apart the stoutest airplane.

So the Comets continued to fly, enhancing British pride and piling up airline profits—until January 10, 1954.

On that day a BOAC Comet departed from Rome's Ciampino Airport bound for London. The aircraft was G-ALYP—Yoke Peter. Before takeoff, Captain Alan Gibson had promised the crew of another BOAC airliner that he would report to them how high the clouds reached above the Mediterranean; if the clouds extended no higher than 15,000 feet, the other plane, which was powered by piston engines, could fly above them and enjoy a smoother trip. At 10:50 a.m. Gibson radioed the Rome airport that he was breaking through the overcast at 26,000 feet en route to his planned cruising altitude of 36,000. One minute later, he began a transmission to the second BOAC airliner below, registration G-ALHJ.

"George How Jig from George Yoke Peter," the message started. "Did you get my . . ." And then, silence. Captain Gibson never completed his message. Less than a minute after he was interrupted, Italian fishermen near the island of Elba saw the remains of his airplane plunge flaming from the clouds into the sea. Yoke Peter, six crew members and 29 passengers had perished.

In England, BOAC's chairman, Sir Miles Thomas, was shocked; neither he nor anyone else familiar with the airplane could do more than speculate about what had happened above 26,000 feet to destroy the Comet. Nor could Sir Miles wait for crash detectives to solve the mystery. Less than 40 hours after the Elba disaster, he voluntarily grounded his airline's entire fleet of seven Comets. "As a measure of prudence," his cautiously worded announcement said, "the normal Comet passenger services are being temporarily suspended to enable minute and unhurried technical examination to be carried out at London Airport." Three jetliners were in England when the grounding order was issued. The remaining four, scattered through the BOAC system, were ferried home carrying only mail.

As soon as the accident had been reported, the Ministry of Civil Aviation's Accident Investigation Branch launched an inquiry. Less than 24 hours later, a parallel investigation began under the supervision of a hastily organized committee composed of representatives from

Test pilot John Cunningham (right) discusses the Comet prototype with two giants of jet aviation. At left is Sir Frank Whittle, pioneer developer of the turbojet; beside him stands Frank Halford, designer of the Comet's Ghost engines, which can be seen buried in the plane's wing.

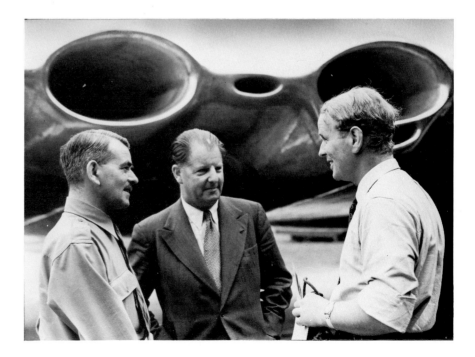

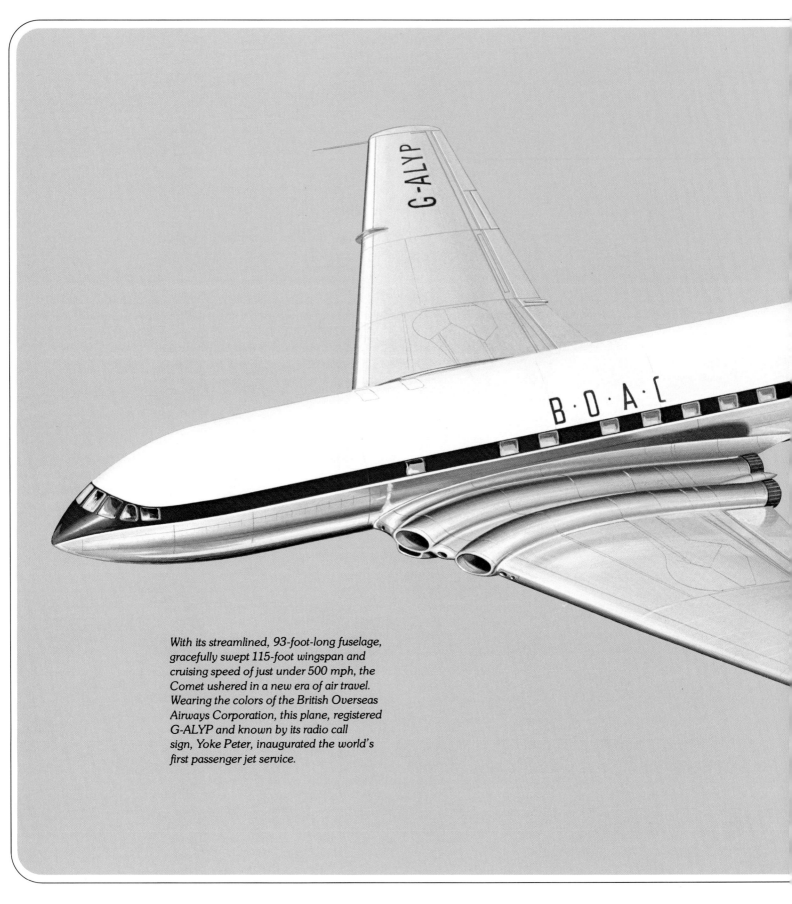

With its streamlined, 93-foot-long fuselage, gracefully swept 115-foot wingspan and cruising speed of just under 500 mph, the Comet ushered in a new era of air travel. Wearing the colors of the British Overseas Airways Corporation, this plane, registered G-ALYP and known by its radio call sign, Yoke Peter, inaugurated the world's first passenger jet service.

Great Britain's wonder plane

When the de Havilland Comet began commercial service in 1952, it created an immediate sensation—and considerable alarm among observers on the other side of the Atlantic: "Whether we like it or not," said the editor of *American Aviation Magazine,* "the British are giving the U.S. a drubbing in jet transport."

And indeed this was the case. The Comet's four 4,500-pound-thrust turbojet engines, developed from designs produced during the 1930s by British inventor Frank Whittle, made the plane the fastest commercial transport of its day. A fully pressurized fuselage enabled it to fly passengers comfortably through the thin air of the stratosphere, eight miles up, where jet engines operate most efficiently. And wing tanks for 7,500 gallons of fuel gave it a range of 1,750 miles—more than twice the distance U.S. experts then thought possible.

Passengers were seated four abreast in the Comet's air-conditioned cabin. The plush forward compartment could seat eight around two tables used for tea, cocktails and meals, while the aft section held 28 travelers in recliner seats.

The vibration-free jet engines—and the fact that the aircraft flew well above most turbulence—made for a marvelously smooth ride. "To compare it with an ordinary plane is like contrasting sailing with motorboating," wrote BOAC president Sir Miles Thomas in the London *Sunday Times.* And one passenger bestowed what was perhaps the ultimate compliment after her first flight. Asked for her impression of the Comet, she replied unself-consciously: "I fell asleep."

BOAC, de Havilland and the British Air Registration Board, which had granted the Comet its airworthiness certificate.

Unfortunately, the sleuths had little to go on. The Italian fishermen, rushing to the scene of the accident, recovered 15 bodies, which were sent to a morgue for autopsy. The British Admiralty organized a salvage operation a week after the crash, but raising Yoke Peter from 500 feet of water—if this feat could be accomplished at all—would take luck and considerable time.

In the absence of hard evidence, speculation abounded. Sabotage came to mind quickly and was infinitely more palatable as a cause for the tragedy than the idea of a fatal flaw in the aircraft. If sabotage was eliminated, the next most logical explanation seemed to be that a turbine blade had snapped off and ruptured a fuel tank, causing an explosion. Turbine blades failed so rarely, however, that this explanation seemed unlikely. Other theories ranged from a breakup in severe turbulence, sometimes encountered in clear skies, to an explosion of fuel vapor in an empty tank.

Sir Victor Tait, BOAC's operations director, made one further suggestion: that metal fatigue had somehow weakened the fuselage, allow-

Near Calcutta, a BOAC ground party searches debris of a Comet for bodies of 43 passengers killed in a crash on the first anniversary of the liner's maiden flight, May 2, 1953. The jet apparently broke up in a thunderstorm, strewing wreckage across an eight-mile area.

Brought to the island of Elba by fishing boats, the bodies of 15 victims of the Yoke Peter crash are loaded onto a flatbed truck for removal to the local morgue. A surgeon who examined them noted, "They showed no look of terror. Death must have come without warning."

ing the air pressure inside to burst it like a balloon. It was true that, during testing, the Comet prototype had developed a fatigue crack in the wing after the equivalent of only 6,700 hours of flying time. But the flaw had been corrected before the airliner went into production. Besides, Yoke Peter had accumulated only 3,682 hours of flight time before crashing and an airliner with less than 4,000 hours on the airframe is considered virtually brand-new and hardly a candidate for metal fatigue.

But unless Yoke Peter could be exhumed from its watery grave off Elba, the crash investigators could neither confirm nor deny any hypothesis. Taking the only course open to them, they guessed at the cause of the accident. After examining the grounded Comets and studying their plans in detail, they recommended 50 modifications that they were certain would solve the problem, whatever it was.

The principal fixes were the installation of armor-plated shields between the engines and fuel tanks, reinforcement of fuel lines, extra fire detectors, new smoke detectors and improved safeguards against the accumulation of hydrogen, an explosive by-product of battery operation. In effect, the committee weighed all possibilities covering mid-air fire and explosion and tried to apply preventives for each.

On February 4, 1954, Sir Miles Thomas announced that BOAC had accepted the investigators' suggestions and 47 days later the modified Comets began flying again. The first to take off did so with every seat filled, once more underlining the public's confidence in the jet.

Even as the Comets were undergoing corrective surgery, salvage vessels of the Royal Navy, using sonar, underwater television cameras and divers to direct massive grappling hooks, had begun the difficult search for Yoke Peter's twisted carcass. Initially, the quest yielded nothing but disappointment. Once, what appeared to be the fuselage turned out to be a freighter sunk during World War I. On another occasion, a television camera produced an unsettling image of a woman's face; it proved to be part of an ancient stone statue.

But by the end of February, the Navy had retrieved a large section of Yoke Peter's tail, plus skin from the rear fuselage, several seats and the two sections of fuselage containing the lavatories and the galley, complete with unbroken bottles of tonic water. Subsequent searching brought up all four engines, the undercarriage, wing spars, huge hunks of fuselage and more of the skin that covered it. On March 31, the grapples hooked Yoke Peter's entire forward section—the cockpit with the flight engineer's body still strapped to the seat and part of the cabin minus the roof.

Recovered wreckage was sent to Britain for examination by scientists of the Royal Aircraft Establishment at Farnborough, headquarters for British aeronautical research, which rendered technical aid to the Ministry of Civil Aviation's Accident Investigation Branch.

As the remains of Yoke Peter accumulated on the floor of an RAE hangar, the Comet was dealt a second devastating blow. On April 8, 1954, only two weeks and two days after resumption of jet service, another of the BOAC jetliners disappeared.

The aircraft was G-ALYY, Yoke Yoke, on a flight from Rome to Cairo. It was climbing to its assigned altitude of 35,500 feet when radio contact suddenly ceased. There were no eyewitnesses this time—the accident occurred at night—but five bodies, two seats and a handful of personal effects were found bobbing in the sea near the volcanic island of Stromboli.

For a second time in little more than three months, the Comets were grounded. As shaken as anyone by the second crash was Britain's Prime Minister, Sir Winston Churchill, who decreed that the cause must be discovered no matter what the effort cost, either in funds or manpower. For this was no ordinary crash probe; at stake was the reputation of Britain's aircraft industry and the role of the jet in air travel.

To lead the search for the Comet's killer, the Cabinet appointed Sir Arnold Hall, the calm, pipe-smoking director of the RAE. All British aviation regarded Hall as the classic English "boffin," a scientist with a single-minded concentration that blotted out everything but the task at hand. That Hall and the RAE assumed the dominant role reflected both the importance of the inquiry and its complexity. The Royal Aircraft Establishment was the embodiment of objective science, and science would have to answer the Comet riddle.

By May 1, the Navy had recovered approximately two thirds of Yoke Peter, an exceptional performance considering that the aircraft had broken into several thousand pieces over 100 square miles of ocean. However, the wreckage was arriving at Farnborough at too slow a pace for Hall—some of it came by battleship. Hall had at his disposal a huge U.S. Air Force cargo plane, loaned to the RAE under a NATO agreement that expressly forbade flying it outside the British Isles. Sir Arnold, a red-tape cutter all his life, dispatched the plane to pick up wreckage without waiting for official permission.

Each scrap that arrived at Farnborough underwent immediate examination, analysis and testing. One of the plane's engines was missing a turbine blade. Perhaps, after all, the theory that a blade had snapped off and pierced a fuel tank was correct. But the lead was false. The experts found the turbine casing intact; the blade had been dislodged by the force of the crash.

Hall guided the inquiry in a different direction. He was intrigued by the fatigue crack that had appeared in the Comet prototype. Wasting no time, he began to examine the possibility, also favored by Dr. Percy B. Walker, head of the Structures Department at Farnborough, that such a crack had doomed Yoke Peter. Hall instructed Walker to build a tank around the fuselage of one of the grounded Comets. The wings protruded from a hole in each side of the tank; gaps were sealed to make the tank watertight. The seats were replaced with ballast to simulate a load of passengers, then tank and cabin were flooded with water.

Dr. Walker's intent was to expose the plane to a lifetime of pressurization cycles by a method that other companies would use to test their new jetliners: Water pressure inside the fuselage was to be raised and lowered while the wings were flexed to simulate flight. If the pressure produced an explosion, the water in the tank would cushion it.

The tank was completed in six weeks, thanks to Sir Arnold's constant prodding, and the Comet's make-believe yet grimly realistic "flights" began. The pressure of the water in the cabin was raised to the eight and a quarter pounds per square inch that would have been the case for a Comet flying above 35,000 feet; it was held there for three minutes and then lowered again while the wings were moved up and down by hydraulic jacks. Dr. Walker calculated that each pressurization cycle in the tank was the equivalent of a three-hour flight. When carried on 24-hours nonstop, such testing would age the Comet nearly 40 times faster than actual airline service.

Meanwhile, the head of RAE's Accidents Investigation Section, Eric Ripley, began hanging the remnants of Yoke Peter on a wooden skeleton in the shape of a Comet. Literally as well as figuratively, the pieces of aviation's greatest jigsaw puzzle were beginning to fit into place.

The wreckage being loosely assembled on Ripley's wooden frame showed mounting evidence that the cabin had failed first. There were blue smears on parts of the tail, and chemical analysis showed that they came from seats. This seemed to indicate that the tail was intact when Yoke Peter broke up above Elba; some force had hurled objects in the cabin against the tail. Scratches on the port wing contained streaks of fuselage paint. Conclusion: The wing was intact when a piece of the fuselage hit it with such power as to brand the wing with paint.

To such irrefutable evidence, Professor Antonio Fornari, the distinguished Italian pathologist who had performed the autopsies on the bodies recovered from Yoke Peter, added still more. Never, he said, had he seen such traumatic injuries—ruptured hearts, torn lungs and fractured skulls. In his opinion, the passengers and crew could only have died "by violent movement and explosive decompression."

RAE scientists had become convinced that the source of the Comet's troubles lay in the fuselage. But they could not say where or how. The answer came on June 24, after the Comet in the water torture tank had been subjected to the equivalent of 9,000 flying hours. Engineers told Sir Arnold Hall that the cabin would no longer hold pressure.

When the tank was drained, the RAE scientists blanched at what they saw. There was a split in the fuselage. It began with a fracture in a corner of an escape hatch window and extended for eight feet, passing directly through a window frame in its path. Examining the window, RAE metallurgists found the telltale discoloration and crystallization of metal fatigue. If this Comet's fuselage had not been wrapped in a watery shock absorber, the entire cabin would have exploded with bomblike force. The two Comets that crashed apparently had done exactly that.

In mid-August, Hall received final corroboration when Italian trawlers brought up a large section of Yoke Peter's cabin roof. Flown to Farnborough and inspected eagerly, it proved to be a virtual carbon copy of the Comet in the tank. A large crack had started in the corner of a navigation window on top of the fuselage and had grown instantly into a wide fracture. This opening, like the escape hatch window, had square corners, a grim reminder of the U.S. Civil Aeronautics Administration's misgivings about the Comet's square windows.

It is axiomatic that no aircraft accident has a single cause. Every crash results from the interplay of several factors that culminates in human or mechanical failure. The square design of the windows, the Comet's ultimate Achilles heel, was but one link in a deadly chain of circumstances that started long before any Comet flew.

To build an airliner whose profitability depended on its ability to fly high and fast, de Havilland had made the plane as lightweight as possible. Had the skin been thicker, it might not have fatigued so quickly. It was no secret at the time that the Comet would have to withstand pressurization stresses no airliner had ever before encountered, and the Comet's fuselage met or surpassed all existing structural standards. But no one at de Havilland—or at the Air Registration Board—had anticipated the effects on the fuselage of the Comet's unusually fast climb to cruising altitude and quick descent to land. Rapid changes in altitude resulted in rapid changes in pressure that flexed the airframe enough to cause metal fatigue at the corners of the windows.

The Comet 1 never carried another passenger. Comet 2 and Comet 3 never flew commercially. And the gallant, pioneering plane's epitaph was written in the coldly impersonal words of the British government's official findings: "The problem of securing an economically satisfactory safe life of the pressure cabin of an aircraft needs more study both in design and by experiment if the highest possible safe structure is to be achieved." That would take another four years.

Caskets of the Comet crash victims are borne through Porto Azzurro, Elba, in a funeral cortege four days after the bodies were retrieved from the sea.

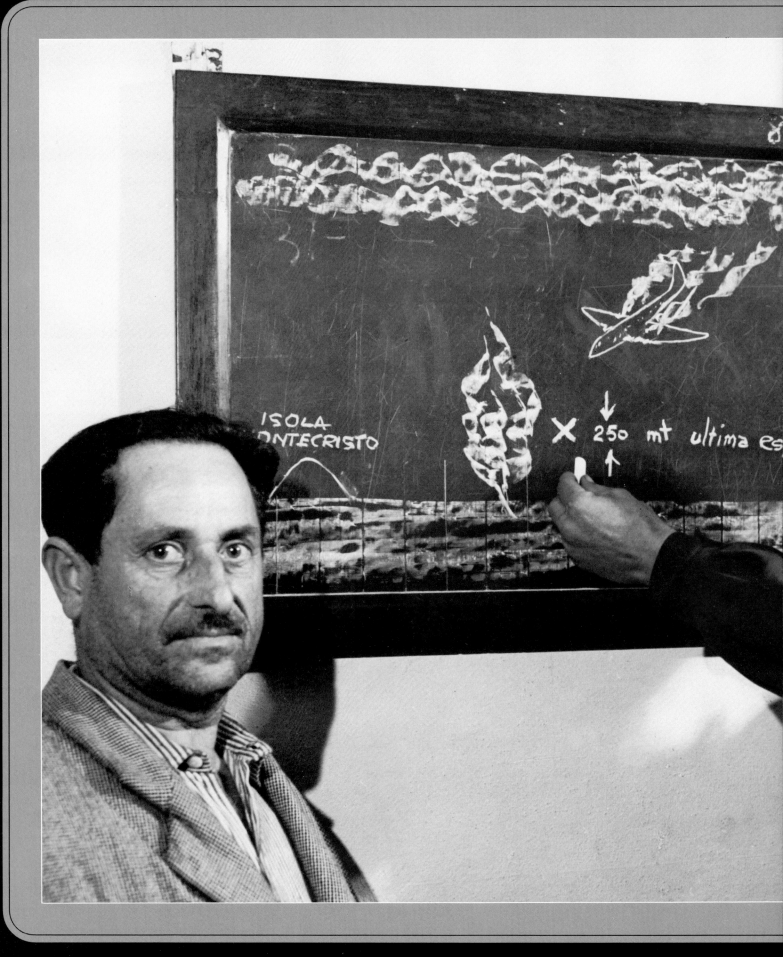

Stalking the Comet's fatal flaw

When in April 1954 Sir Arnold Hall of the Royal Aircraft Establishment at Farnborough, England, was asked to find out why two Comet jet airliners had broken up over the Mediterranean earlier that year, he divided his staff into groups so that it could pursue different lines of inquiry simultaneously and come to a conclusion sooner than might otherwise have been possible. One group not only took a Comet on test flights but simulated flights on the ground, reproducing as closely as possible the conditions under which Yoke Peter and its sister ship, Yoke Yoke, had met disaster. These experiments were intended to eliminate all possible causes save the actual one, thus providing circumstantial evidence of the Comet's fatal flaw.

A second group, like coroners seeking the cause of death in a mutilated victim, pored over the wreckage of Yoke Peter recovered by the Royal Navy. "To achieve a desirable degree of certainty," Sir Arnold said, "it was most important to find the piece that carried the fingerprints of the cause." After reconstructing sections of the jet on a wooden frame at Farnborough, however, the investigators realized that vital parts were still missing.

To guide the salvage crews fishing for the remaining pieces, ingenious tests were conducted using 20 models $1/36$ the size of a Comet. The replicas, designed to disintegrate in mid-air, were taken up 835 feet in a balloon and launched at a velocity of 90 feet per second to represent proportionally Yoke Peter's speed and altitude at the time of the accident. Mathematicians studied the pattern in which the fragments scattered and were able to suggest likely spots on the seabed where major sections of the jet might be found. In a short time, most of the rest of the plane was recovered and the detective work went on.

Italian eyewitnesses recreate in chalk the Comet Yoke Peter's fiery plunge into the sea. "I heard three explosions," one fisherman said. "Then several miles away, I saw a silver thing flash out of the clouds. By the time I got there, all was still again."

An underwater television camera dangles from a ship's pulley. When suspended 20 feet above the seabed, the wide-angle lens could scan a 320-square-foot area.

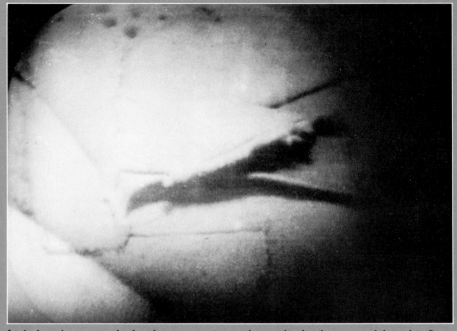

Light from lamps attached to the camera pierces the murky depths to reveal the cabin floor.

From watery grave to aeronautic autopsy

The retrieval of Yoke Peter, said one Royal Navy captain, was simply "a matter of time and luck." It was also a matter of applying the very latest underwater salvage techniques.

Ships equipped with sonar located promising projections on the sea floor and marked the sites with flagged buoys. A salvage vessel dropped anchor near each buoy and lowered an underwater television camera. Whenever something showed up on the screen, an operator in a diving chamber guided the 4½-ton claw of a crane down to retrieve it.

After three months of work, about three fourths of the Comet was brought up and sent to England. All four jet engines were given a clean bill of health, and investigators began a painstaking examination of the rest of the wreckage to determine what had caused the Comet to break up.

An Italian trawler nets a big catch—the first major part of the jet's fuselage to be recovered.

Sailors on the deck of the salvage vessel Sea Salvor glean and hose fragments of Yoke Peter smeared with muck from the sea floor.

Surrounded by villagers, officials make a preliminary inspection of one of the de Havilland Ghost engines on a pier at Portoferraio, Elba.

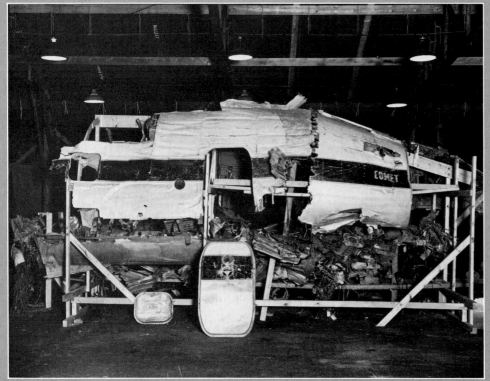

The crew's hatch (center) and equipment bay door beside it lean against Yoke Peter's nose. Absence of fire damage to the forward cabin indicated that it had separated from the burning fuselage in mid-air.

The severed tail—with Speedbird emblem and the call letters G-ALYP intact—rests on a frame. The cabin roof (left) shows a pressure dome formed when the fuselage struck water open-end first.

Yoke Peter, skeletal on a wooden frame, lies ringed

by its skin and contents in a hangar at the Royal Aircraft Establishment in Farnborough. Reassembling it was "like a 3-D jigsaw puzzle," a reporter marveled.

Transformed from posh airliner into flying lab, a Comet under test displays a double row of devices for recording in-flight loads and stresses.

Tempting a tiger at 35,000 feet

Twenty members of Hall's staff volunteered to conduct performance tests in a Comet that were to push the airliner to its limits. "They were going as close to the tiger as possible," said one investigator, "hoping it would not get them."

The jet's seats were removed and the plane was wired with instruments connected to recording machines installed in the forward half of the main cabin.

Because Sir Arnold suspected that the Comet disasters were due to explosive decompression of the passenger cabins, he took the precaution of ordering that the test plane be flown unpressurized, even when at a maximum altitude of 35,000 feet. As a result, the observers and crew had to wear oxygen masks, and several suffered from the bends—severe joint pain caused by nitrogen bubbles in the bloodstream.

To everyone's relief, the Comet went up 50 times without incident. "The test flights covered possibilities which proved negative," Hall said, "but added to the process of isolating the real cause."

Evidence from another experiment—one conducted in the comparative safety of an RAE lab—confirmed Sir Arnold's belief that violent depressurization had destroyed Yoke Peter. A plastic 1/10 scale model, complete with bulkheads, 28 seats and six mannequins, was placed in an evacuation chamber. While the model was pressurized, the exterior pressure was brought to a high-altitude level to duplicate actual flight conditions. A high-speed movie camera captured the result when a section of the cabin roof was blown off with a small explosive charge *(right).*

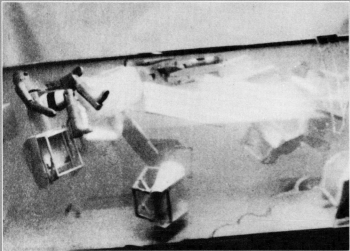

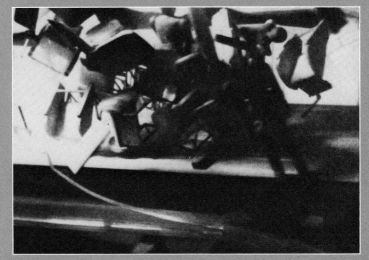

A dramatic sequence of frames showing a model of the Comet's fuselage subjected to explosive decompression reveals how 56 passengers and crewmen met sudden death. "An instantaneous and powerful force in the cabin," Hall said, "threw most of them upwards against the roof."

Shots taken from another angle show a section of the model's roof (top) being blasted off (middle) and the contents being shot through the hole (bottom). "The tube became," said Sir Arnold, referring to the fuselage, "what the layman might describe as a compressed-air gun."

Uncovering the final clue

Months of weeding out possible causes for the disasters left Sir Arnold with one primary suspect: metal fatigue. He decided that the only way to find if such fatigue had caused the crashes was to subject a Comet to untoward strain.

Yoke Uncle, a jet that had flown as long as Yoke Peter, was selected for testing. Workmen built a rubber-lined steel tank around the fuselage. Yoke Uncle was then submerged in water and subjected to pressure changes simulating the effects of a continuous series of three-hour flights. Water pumped in and out of the fuselage caused the difference between interior and exterior pressure to go up and down as if the plane were taking off, flying to 30,000 feet and descending. Hydraulic jacks waggled the wings to reflect actual flying conditions.

The tank was periodically drained, and slowly new evidence accumulated. The pressure changes had pulled rivets through the skin and caused cracks in the fuselage, frame and floor beams. After the equivalent of 3,057 flights, a large split suddenly appeared at the forward escape hatch. Had the jet been aloft, it would have immediately broken up as the pressurized air inside the fuselage forced its way out with explosive effect. The Comet's fatal flaw had been found.

Yoke Uncle, its fuselage submerged in a quarter of a million gallons of water in a 112-foot-long tank, undergoes a fatigue test. Hydraulic rigs in the huts to the left of the Comet controlled pressure within the cabin.

Exterior and interior views of the escape hatch where the cabin first split show that the window stayed in place, but that the metal frame popped out. In flight, such an incident would have destroyed the plane at once.

2
America enters the jet age

In 1950, two years before Yoke Peter's historic maiden flight to Johannesburg, William M. Allen, the president of the Boeing Aircraft Company, went to England to check out the Comet. He was accompanied by Maynard Pennell, Boeing's chief of Preliminary Design, and together they attended the Farnborough Air Show, a major aviation fair held every two years.

Allen and Pennell stood among other luminaries on the grassy slopes overlooking the airfield and awaited the first public appearance of the plane. As the new jetliner approached, not even the metallic timbre of the public address system could muffle the pride in the announcer's voice. "This aircraft," he proclaimed above the murmurs of the awed crowd, "has an unrivaled cruising speed of 490 miles per hour at 35,000 to 42,000 feet. An aircraft with extraordinary commercial capabilities . . ."

The Comet screamed over the field at full throttle, only a few hundred feet off the ground, then curved up sharply and effortlessly like a huge silver knife slicing through the sky. Allen turned to his British host.

"Appears to be a fine airplane," he commented graciously. But in the mind of this competitive businessman, the seeds of challenge had been sown. At dinner that night, he asked Pennell what he thought of the Comet.

"It's a very good airplane," Pennell said.

"Do you think we could build one as good?"

"Better," Pennell assured him. "Much better."

Back at headquarters in Seattle, Allen, Pennell and the Boeing brain trust began to assess the prospects for a Boeing success in the jetliner field. Of the five major U.S. airliner manufacturers, Boeing alone possessed experience in building large jet aircraft. Douglas and Lockheed had produced between them nearly a dozen types of jet fighters; Convair and Martin had built only experimental jets. But the six-engined Boeing B-47 jet bomber had been flying for nearly two years and was in full production; an even larger, eight-engined jet bomber, the B-52, was only two years away from roll-out and initial test flights. To be sure, these were military airplanes, but much of the experience ac-

Emerging from its hangar, Boeing's $16 million 707 prototype makes its public debut as America's first jet transport one month after Britain's ill-fated Comet was grounded.

quired in producing them would apply to creating a civilian transport.

There was no evidence that Boeing's American rivals were doing much more than daydream about building passenger jets. In Burbank, California, where Lockheed's Clarence L. "Kelly" Johnson ran his Advanced Development Projects Staff out of a cluster of offices known as Kelly's Skunk Works, preliminary design studies were under way on several jetliner concepts. The most promising was for a double-decked plane with four turbojets mounted on each side of the fuselage near the tail. But with the exception of the talented denizens of the Skunk Works, no one at Lockheed took this or the other schemes seriously.

In Santa Monica, a few miles to the south, Douglas had no specifics on paper. As early as 1943, company officials had sounded out a number of airlines on a plan to build a small, jet-powered flying laboratory that would provide some insights into the feasibility of a commercial jet, but the idea had received a cool reception. So the company continued its concentration instead on the profitable business of producing DC-6s and DC-7s, the world's best-selling airliners. At Convair and Martin, both busily engaged in cranking out twin-engined piston transports, the notion of building jet airliners sparked not much more of a response.

Boeing knew the risks involved in launching an airliner. Though the company enjoyed a reputation second to none as a builder of heavy bombers, it ranked far behind Douglas and Lockheed in the airliner field. Four times in its four-decade history Boeing had attempted to gain transport supremacy but had been dogged by failure. First there was the Model 80, a three-engined, fabric-covered biplane that carried 12 passengers in what was unusual luxury for the 1920s—the craft boasted upholstered seats, reading lights and the first stewardesses on any American airliner. Introduced in 1928 on the Chicago-San Francisco route by Boeing Air Transport, the plane proved to be sturdy and reliable. But it could not match the popularity of the all-metal Ford Tri-motor monoplane, which had appeared two years earlier, and it was very slow. One wag said that "when you saw it on the horizon coming into Great Falls from Butte, you still had time to drive to the downtown post office, pick up the mail, and get back to the field before it landed." Only a handful of Model 80s were ever built.

Next came the 247, a twin-engined, all-metal monoplane. It entered service in 1933 hailed as the world's fastest airliner, and it was—for almost a year. Then virtually overnight, the newer, faster and bigger Douglas DC-2 rendered the 247 obsolete.

Boeing's third try involved a prewar transport, the B-307 Stratoliner, which had the distinction of being the world's first airliner with a pressurized cabin. The Stratoliner bore more than a passing resemblance to Boeing's B-17 Flying Fortress; its dirigible-shaped fuselage had been mated to the wings and tail of the famous bomber. World War II made the B-17 a legend, but it destroyed any chance of commercial success for the Stratoliner. Airlines, eager to keep up with the times, showed no enthusiasm for a plane that had been designed before the War.

Inside Boeing's wind tunnel, top engineer Edward C. Wells looks over a 707 test model built to scale, one of four that required some 5,000 shop hours to develop. This early design, featuring a pair of low-slung pods with two turbines each, was later modified to include four separate engine pods.

Boeing's response was to come up with the Stratocruiser, a commercial version of its new four-engined military tanker, the C-97, purchased by the U.S. Air Force for in-flight refueling of long-range bombers. The Stratocruiser was loved by passengers and hated by the airlines. The flying public appreciated its roomy comfort; the Stratocruiser had two decks, a cocktail lounge on the lower level—and a few models even had sleeping berths. But the plane was unreliable and expensive to operate. In competition with the new, faster Douglas DC-6 and Lockheed Constellation, both four-engined airliners with pressurized cabins, the Stratocruiser turned out to be an economic disappointment for Boeing. Between 1944 and 1950, only 55 were built; in that same time, Douglas produced 175 DC-6s and Lockheed built 232 Constellations.

With the delivery of the final Stratocruiser, Boeing seemed to be out of the commercial transport business entirely. Yet Boeing's president Allen, a lawyer who had risen to the top of the company hierarchy by virtue of his skill in contract negotiations, was only too aware of an unpleasant fact of life: Boeing would never prosper if it attempted to live off military business alone.

The decision was made to go ahead with the jetliner. Allen and his team inaugurated comprehensive design studies. Almost from the start, they thought big. Though Allen and Pennell had been impressed with the Comet's performance, they regarded its relatively small size as a drawback. Boeing's engineers were convinced that to be as economical to operate as a piston-engined plane, a jetliner would have to carry at least twice as many passengers.

To design a prototype, Boeing engineers first searched through their blueprints to see if they could put together a jetliner from wings, tails and fuselages already on hand. The initial design carried the designation

Model 367-64, the 64th variation in the Stratocruiser series, and it did resemble the older plane in its rather fat, if larger, fuselage and its modestly sweptback wings, each fitted with a single pod containing two jet engines.

The engine arrangement had been copied from Boeing's jet bombers, but the designers were not happy with it. Safety was their main consideration: If one engine exploded, it could easily damage the adjoining one. They settled therefore on four separate engine pods, two slung under each wing. This would not only solve the safety problem but would distribute the engines' weight (at 3,500 pounds, each engine was almost half again as heavy as Lindbergh's *Spirit of St. Louis).* While wind tunnel tests confirmed the wisdom of the arrangement—air currents flowed undisturbed past the engines and across the wings—they also revealed that the whalelike fuselage would create prohibitive air resistance, slowing the aircraft and making it uneconomical to fly. The designers now set about changing the fuselage's shape.

Although modifications were swinging the aircraft increasingly away from the Stratocruiser concept, Boeing continued to number the new designs as if they still bore resemblance to the old piston-engined plane, designating the last of the series Model 367-80. "It was partially a bit of camouflage," an official was later to admit. "We wanted people to believe we were going the Stratocruiser route with the jet. It was quite early that in-house, we began calling it something else." They called it the 707—the 707th design in the long line of airplane concepts at Boeing.

Whatever the jet's final form, Allen insisted that the 707 must be able to serve as both a commercial transport and, with only minor alteration, as a military tanker. He knew from Boeing's experience with the Stratoliner and the B-17 that there was economy in building a plane with interchangeable components. Allen also knew that the Air Force soon would be in the market for a new jet tanker. Boeing's C-97 could not fly high enough to refuel B-47 and B-52 jet bombers at their operating altitudes. If the Air Force bought the plane, putting its stamp of approval on it, the airlines would be bound to flock to the jet.

There was some evidence that the airlines were interested in a passenger jet. Early in 1952, before Boeing's work on the 707 became common knowledge, United Air Lines embarked on an experiment called Operation *Paper Jet* to determine whether 550-mile-per-hour jets could mesh with much slower piston-engined traffic. Daily, for more than a year, theoretical aircraft completed two round-trip flights coast-to-coast—on paper. They were assumed to cover the distance nonstop, fueled with mathematical computations and graphs intended to simulate a real operation. On paper at least the flights were an unqualified success. But at the time only Pan American World Airways had the money to buy jets and it had already placed orders with de Havilland for Comets. United and the rest of the large U.S. airlines were mortgaged up to their flaps, having spent some $600 million, as of January 1, 1952,

"The biggest blunder"

When the DC-8 was still on the drawing boards and the 707 existed only in prototype, Britain again had a chance to seize the lead in commercial aviation with the Vickers jet, a giant plane offering the advantage of transatlantic range.

Designed for military transport as well as airline service, the V.1000 was to carry 100 passengers 2,900 miles at a cruising speed of 500 mph. But the development cost proved too high for the RAF, and BOAC could not assume the expense alone. So the jet, 80 per cent completed, was scrapped in 1955 in a move the project director would later call "the biggest blunder of all."

A model of the V.1000 clearly shows the distinctive shape of its wings.   *Construction halted, the V.1000 sits abandoned in the Vickers shop.*

on hundreds of new DC-6s, Constellations, Stratocruisers, Convairs and Martins. And the Air Force had yet to persuade Congress to appropriate money for replacing the C-97.

If Boeing wanted to see the 707 fly, it could not count on help from the airlines; it would have to pay the development costs itself. On April 22, 1952—just 10 days before the Comet began carrying passengers—the Boeing board of directors authorized the expenditure of $15 million, one fourth of the company's net worth, for the development of a prototype. It was a step into the void. Should the Air Force or the airlines decline to purchase the plane, Boeing would face possible bankruptcy.

With the company's future at stake, Boeing set about the immensely complex task of creating the best airliner it knew how to build. The design was refined in more than 4,240 hours of aerodynamic testing in wind tunnels. The entire airframe was constructed on a fail-safe principle—no structural component could give out without another component assuming the additional burden. The wings, fuselage and tail were exposed to all kinds of stress; one wing snapped only after it was subjected to loads more than 110 per cent above the maximum stress it would encounter under the most severe flight conditions. Triple-strength round windows, plug-type doors that sealed tighter as the plane flew higher, spot welds instead of rivets for greater strength—these and other features would make the 707 the strongest airliner ever built.

Perhaps the wisest decision—and certainly the most prescient—involved the skin of the aircraft. Months before the Comet's tragic vulnerability to explosive decompression became known, Boeing engineers specified aluminum for the skin that was four and one half times as

Christening the 707 prototype at its roll-out in May 1954, Bertha Boeing, wife of the company founder, breaks a bottle of champagne against the jet's nose, much to the delight of president William Allen. The day was a special triumph for Allen, who had boldly risked the firm's future on the development of a commercial jet.

thick as the Comet's, to resist tearing. Moreover, at frequent intervals, they welded to the inside of the skin "tear stoppers" made of titanium, a metal as light as aluminum but stronger than steel. Thus, wherever a metal-fatigue rupture might start, it would soon encounter a titanium strip blocking its deadly path. But there was little chance that the skin would crack. Boeing put a 707 fuselage through 50,000 pressurization cycles, and still the vital sheath of metal remained intact.

The finished plane was immense. It weighed 160,000 pounds. The fuselage, 128 feet long, stretched eight feet farther than the distance covered by Wilbur Wright on man's first powered flight, and the nose gear alone was heavier than the Wright brothers' Flyer.

The 707 made its first flight on July 15, 1954, with A. M. "Tex" Johnston, Boeing's chief test pilot, at the controls. For an hour and 24 minutes, Johnston put it through its paces. "She wanted to climb like a rocket," he reported excitedly upon landing. The Boeing people were overjoyed; they knew they had a viable jet airliner to sell to any comers and a jump on potential American competitors.

But for all its initial success, the 707 was far from a perfect plane. It could not, for example, carry enough fuel to fly a full payload nonstop across the Atlantic. And test flights quickly disclosed that it actually was underpowered. Though its Pratt & Whitney JT3P engines were almost three times as powerful as the Comet's Ghost turbojets, the 707 weighed half again as much as the Comet. When heavily loaded in hot weather, it required so much runway to become airborne that it would be unsafe to operate from most airports. To solve the problem hundreds of gallons of cold water were injected into the engine's air intakes during the takeoff roll. The water lowered the engine temperatures, making the air within denser so that more fuel could be burned. The result was 1,000 pounds more thrust at the moment it was needed most. Eventually engines of greater power would be substituted for the JT-3s.

Other problems—some of them disconcerting even to an experi-

A. M. "Tex" Johnston, Boeing's colorful chief test pilot, checks out the 707's cockpit shortly before taking the jet aloft on its maiden flight. Johnston was so bedazzled by the plane's performance, goes the story, that when he returned to the pilots' ready room to change his clothes he marched into the shower still wearing his cowboy boots.

enced hand such as Johnston—arose during the exhaustive program of test flights necessary before the 707 could be declared safe. After conducting a series of runway braking tests, Johnston and his crew climbed to 22,000 feet for other tests when they heard a sound "like someone shooting off both barrels of a 12-gauge shotgun in the cockpit." An F-86 Sabrejet was being used as a chase plane, observing the tests from close by; its pilot radioed Johnston that black smoke was pouring from his wheel-well doors. Johnston lowered the landing gear and the chase pilot reported that some of the jet's 10 tires were on fire. Johnston extinguished the flames by increasing speed and managed to land the jet in one piece.

Boeing's engineers soon discovered that the 707's brakes were at fault. During the braking tests before the flight, they had become overheated and caused the tires to burst, then catch fire. Though the circumstances that caused the incident were unlikely to be duplicated under normal operating conditions, Boeing redesigned the brakes to dissipate heat more quickly.

Johnston had another scare when he was diving the big jet at its maximum speed. The plane suddenly began to shudder. Johnston slowed down to stop it before the plane became uncontrollable. "Appreciable vibration" was his laconic report upon landing. That was more than an understatement; the jolting had loosened the flight engineer's instrument panel from its latches. The trouble was traced to the failure of a small component in the tail, intended to keep the rudder from shaking the airplane to pieces at high speed.

Interspersed among the test flights were demonstration rides for Air Force officials and airline executives from around the world. For most it was their first exposure to the silky-smooth power of jet flight and there was no better tour conductor than Johnston. He particularly enjoyed showing off the 707 to senior airline pilots, who were allowed to take over the controls.

When Johnston himself put the plane through its paces he could do so dramatically. Once he was asked to make a low pass over the Gold Cup Hydroplane Boat Races on Seattle's Lake Washington. This was Allen's idea, his way of impressing members of the Aircraft Industries Association, who were aboard a specially chartered yacht. As the 707 screamed into view, Allen's composure dissolved. He watched aghast as Johnston put the only 707 in existence through two complete barrel rolls at high altitude, then dived and rolled the huge plane again, directly over the yacht. It was an impressive demonstration of the plane's structural strength, but for a heart-stopping moment Allen had visions of a $16 million investment splitting at every rivet and seam. Later he is supposed to have chastised Johnston. But the industry officials who had witnessed the stunts gave the 707 valuable word-of-mouth advertising.

Boeing, of course, needed all the publicity it could get for the new plane and it went to great pains to promote the 707—and to remove any doubts people might have about flying in a jet. One sales tool used was a movie entitled *Operation Guillotine*. It offered visual proof that the Comet's problem would not afflict the 707. The film, shown to every potential customer beginning in 1955, opened with a shot of a pressurized airliner fuselage, structurally similar to the Comet's, mounted on a platform. Above it, like swords of Damocles, hung two huge steel blades. In slow motion, the blades dropped, piercing the fuselage. At the two points of penetration, the metal skin began to split and curl outward, faster and farther until suddenly the entire fuselage burst like a ripe pea pod, ejecting seats, dummies representing passengers, overhead bins, even the cabin floor.

The camera then focused on a 707 fuselage reinforced with titanium tear stoppers. Five big blades sliced through the skin, and there was never a person in the audience who did not wince in anticipation. Nothing happened. Little puffs of air could be heard escaping from the wounds, and that was it—no disintegration, no explosive decompression. Plainly, if a tear occurred in a 707, the pilot would have plenty of time for a descent to a safe altitude as passengers donned automatically deployed oxygen masks.

Boeing signed up its first customer in March 1955; the U.S. Air Force ordered a fleet of 29 jet tankers. There were no civilian orders yet, to be sure, but the military contract served as a psychological as well as financial boost. Nor was the Air Force purchase of the 707s lost on the apparently slumbering giant to the south. In early June, 1955, Douglas Aircraft announced that it would design and produce a jet transport, the DC-8. The race was on.

In many ways, Douglas was accepting greater risks than Boeing had when it undertook the 707 two years earlier. Douglas would not have a military contract to help defray development costs. Nor would there be time to create a prototype. The first DC-8 would have to be almost perfect the day it flew, and it would have to be better than the 707.

Douglas had not been asleep all the time. Only a month after

The Tu-104 jet's twin engines provided up to 30,000 pounds of thrust and gave the plane a cruising speed of 500 mph.

A bomber with seats

During an early thaw in the Cold War, the first Soviet jet transport to be seen in the West, Aeroflot's Tupolev 104, roared into London on a diplomatic mission. Arriving in March 1956, at a time when the Comet 1 was grounded and the 707 was not yet carrying passengers, the so-called Red jet was described by the press as "a veiled threat," "a smug boast" and "a sneering challenge to Western jet development." London's *Daily Mail* even worried that the Tu-104 was "more advanced than anything likely to be available in Britain or the U.S. for at least three years."

Adapted from the Russians' Tu-16 Badger bomber, the jetliner represented an odd marriage of warplane and commercial transport. Its flight deck resembled the bomber's, with the navigator located in the glass-encased nose where the bombardier sat in the Badger. In contrast, the four cabins aft were almost Edwardian in their décor, with lacy curtains hanging over windows in the partitions and porcelain figurines lining glass-fronted cabinets in the buffet. The jet also featured two clothes closets, three commodious lavatories and lounge seating, and it provided meals cooked to order. But because the Tu-104 could carry only 50 passengers and was a gulper of fuel, Western aircraft makers were quick to agree that it posed no real threat to them. Not surprisingly, the Tu-104 never broke into the world jet market.

But the 250 or so that flew for Aeroflot were tremendously successful within the vast Soviet Union, where they slashed flight times between such distant cities as Moscow and Irkutsk from 14 hours to five and a half.

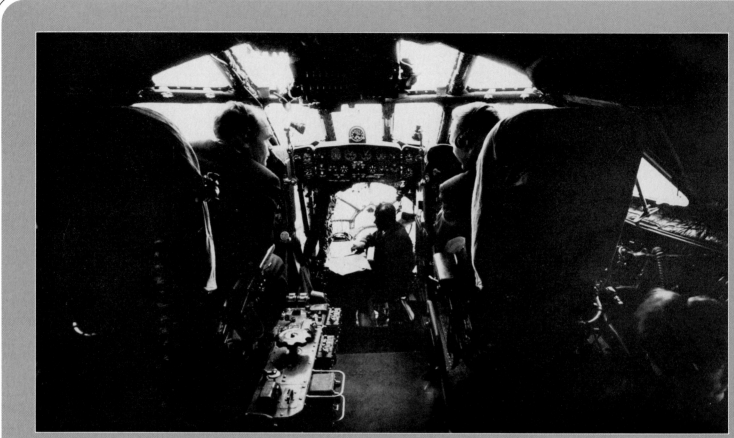

The Tu-104 cockpit, unorthodox for an airliner, features a wide aisle, overhead autopilot and fans for keeping pilot and copilot cool.

Passengers play chess beside a model of the Tu-104. The plane operated most efficiently at 33,000 feet.

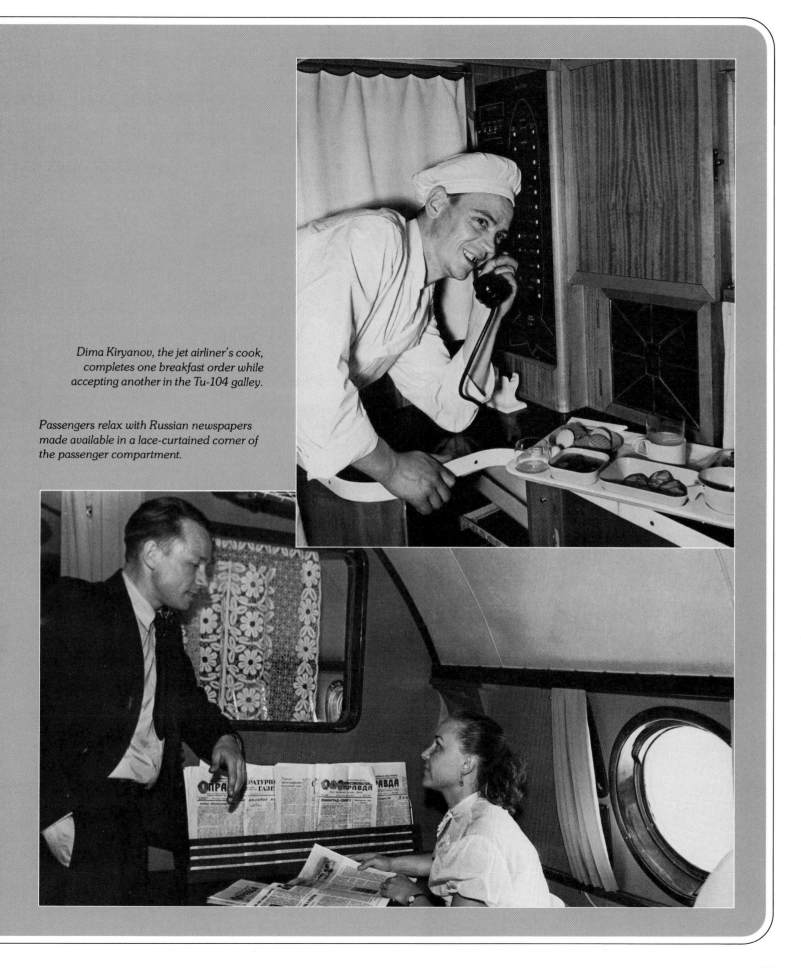

Dima Kiryanov, the jet airliner's cook, completes one breakfast order while accepting another in the Tu-104 galley.

Passengers relax with Russian newspapers made available in a lace-curtained corner of the passenger compartment.

Boeing's board of directors had approved the construction of the 707 in 1952, Douglas established a secret Special Project Office so hush-hush that only a handful of executives knew of its work, which was to draw up specifications for the DC-8. Later that year, Douglas invited the airlines to Santa Monica for the unveiling of a full-scale mock-up of the result, a 560-mile-per-hour plane that, the visitors were told, could be in service by 1958—providing they demonstrated their interest with orders. To the disappointment of the Special Project Office, the airlines exhibited far greater interest in Douglas' plans for the ultimate in piston transports: the DC-7, an enlarged DC-6 with nonstop transcontinental and transoceanic range.

Douglas had undertaken the DC-7 project in 1952 at the instigation of American Airlines' president C. R. Smith, who wanted a plane that could fly farther and faster than the Lockheed Constellation used by his competition, Trans World Airlines and Eastern Air Lines. And Douglas provided such a plane. The DC-7s carried a power plant touted by Douglas' engineers as "the most efficient large piston engine ever developed"—the innovative Wright R-3350 turbo-compound radial engine. The R-3350 used the power in the hot exhaust from its 18 cylinders to drive a turbine on the propeller shaft. The result was a substantial increase in power without the penalty of greater fuel consumption; it enabled the DC-7 to cruise at 350 miles per hour with a 20 per cent greater range than the DC-6.

Diverted by the success of the DC-7, Douglas did little work on the DC-8, even after rumors of Boeing's 707 were confirmed. It took a visit from representatives of Pan American World Airways in 1955 to awaken Donald Douglas to the reality that the jet age was about to pass his company by. Pan Am had agreed to purchase Comets from Britain, but the deal fell through when the plane was permanently grounded, and the airline went shopping for another plane. Fresh from a demonstration flight aboard the 707, Pan Am executives descended on Santa Monica to persuade Douglas to take up Boeing's gauntlet; a better airplane might emerge from spirited competition between builders than from a de facto Boeing monopoly. Douglas knew what effect a Pan Am order for the 707 would have on an industry that traditionally played follow-the-leader in equipment. His firm would be condemned to eating Boeing's exhaust forever.

There was no time to lose. The company needed orders for the DC-8, but all it had to offer were blueprints, sketches, theoretical performance specifications, the results of wind tunnel tests on models and an outmoded, three-year-old mock-up. Who could be expected to put a deposit on a paper airplane?

In one respect, at least, Boeing's lead gave Douglas an advantage. Though the 707 might be only a prototype, it was nevertheless a successful one, and because of the fortune the plane had cost, and the risk it had entailed to the company, Boeing would be unlikely to spend more money on design changes for some time to come. Douglas, on the other

Behind a tableful of earlier commercial successes, Donald Douglas shows off a model of the DC-8, his company's last-minute entry into the jet sweepstakes. Starting a year after the 707's roll-out, Douglas plunged into building the DC-8, pouring one billion dollars into the project.

hand, could benefit from what it saw as the 707's drawbacks. For one thing, it could provide a wider cabin so that more seats could be used. Better yet, it could build a plane with a greater range. Boeing, admitted Douglas salesmen, would have earlier deliveries, but wait about a year, potential customers were told, for a superior product.

Douglas had to build the DC-8 right on the first try; there would be no time—or money—for a second attempt. Thus, the DC-8's development program was meticulous. No fewer than 42 shapes for cabin windows were tested before one was selected; it was not only as strong as the 707's but it was a third larger. The window frames were subjected to almost 120,000 pressurization cycles to prove their durability. Three thousand employees of various heights and weights were sent through evacuation doors before a design was chosen that would make an emergency exit as speedy for a 300-pound man as for a 75-pound child. As a test of windshield strength, the bodies of four-pound chickens were

fired from a compressed-air gun at 460 miles an hour to simulate mid-air collisions with birds.

Then what Douglas had been hoping for happened. On October 13, 1955, before a single DC-8 had been built, the company received its first order. Pan Am announced it would buy 25 DC-8s—and 20 Boeing 707s—at a total cost of $269 million.

Boeing's president Allen was floored. His beloved 707, which had been breaking every point-to-point speed record on the books, now was five airline orders behind a jet that did not even exist. And worse was yet to come; 12 days later, United Air Lines announced it had signed a contract for 30 of Douglas' planes—a contract that only two weeks earlier Boeing had figured was in its pocket. But United technicians had built a mock-up of a hybrid jetliner cabin; one side had the dimensions of a 707 interior and the other those of a DC-8. William A. Patterson, United's diminutive and dynamic chief, had been leaning toward Boeing except for one factor—the DC-8's fuselage was 15 inches wider than the 707's. These few extra inches would allow six passengers instead of five to sit in a row; to attempt the same feat in the 707 would have cramped customers in skimpy seats separated by an uncomfortably narrow aisle.

Boeing refused Patterson's request to widen the 707 cabin, but it did

Drumming up orders at a convention in Seattle, Boeing president William Allen, second from left, uses a model to show distinctive features of the 707 to potential buyers from the airlines. Lacking a sales staff familiar with the virtues of the jet, Allen took to the road himself.

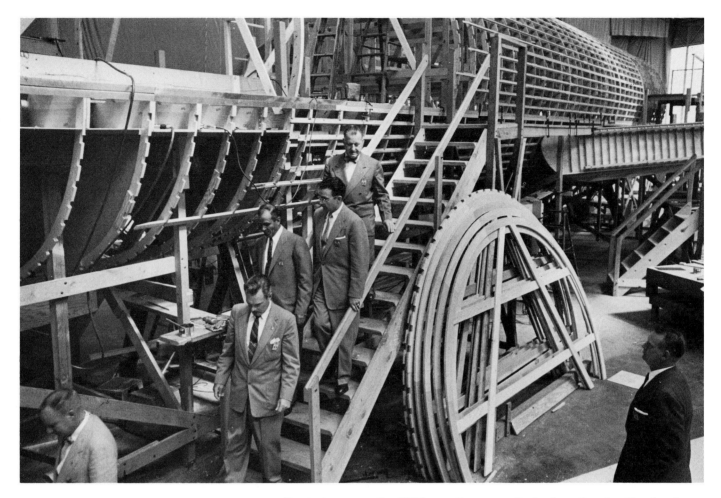

An American Airlines delegation led by flight director Walt Braznell steps down from a DC-8 mock-up in Douglas' hangars. With little more than the mock-up to sell against the already proven Boeing prototype, Douglas salesmen emphasized the DC-8's greater seating capacity and longer range.

offer to increase the 707's seating capacity by lengthening the fuselage, a much simpler task than widening it. However, Boeing could not stretch the plane enough to match the number of seats in the DC-8. So United bought Douglases, even though it would have to wait at least a year to get them. Suddenly Boeing had fewer than half the orders that Douglas had. The airlines appeared to be stampeding to Douglas, and Boeing could discern ghosts of failures past returning to haunt it. If the course of events was not altered, the 707 could become another 247 or Stratocruiser and the company might go under.

More bad news came from Pan Am's Juan Trippe, who bluntly told Allen why he had bought so many DC-8s. Pan Am, he said, considered the 707 merely an interim airplane, purchased solely because of its earlier delivery date. The airline's own experts preferred the DC-8. Optional engines—Pratt & Whitney JT-4s, with 45 per cent more power than the 707's JT-3s—and greater lift would allow the Douglas jet to carry enough fuel for the nonstop transatlantic range the 707 lacked. Boeing had no alternative but to redesign its plane.

The first decision was to widen the fuselage by 16 inches, an inch more than the DC-8. The second was to offer a second, higher-powered version of the 707, known as the Intercontinental. It would be eight feet longer than the standard model and would have a 12 foot greater

*With Donald Douglas Sr. (right) and Jr.
peering from the cockpit, the first DC-8 is
rolled out on April 9, 1958. The plane
resembled the 707 but for the sweepback of
the wings and the air ducts under its nose.*

wingspan and 1,200 miles of additional range. Pan Am took one look at the new design and changed its 20-plane order; it would still accept six of the shorter 707s, but the other 14, plus an additional three aircraft, would be Intercontinentals.

Boeing had turned the tables on Douglas. To be sure, Boeing remained far behind on orders, but now it had two airliners that it could pair with customers' special needs. Douglas stood pat with its single version of the DC-8. It had no choice. The crash project to design the jetliner had "all but wrecked the company," said Art Raymond, Douglas' chief engineer, years later.

Boeing's new-found flexibility attracted orders from unexpected quarters. Qantas, Australia's biggest airline, had flown Douglas airliners since DC-3 days, but for its first jets, the airline switched to Boeing. What clinched the deal was Boeing's willingness to build for Qantas the shorter-bodied 707-138, even though no other airline would ever buy one. Boeing won Braniff Airways' business with the same flexibility. Braniff needed a high-powered jet for the high-altitude South American airports that the airline served. Boeing's response was to install JT-4 engines on the standard 707.

Now there was a stampede by the airlines to buy jets. American Airlines signed for 30 standard 707s and took an option for 20 more. Eastern, KLM, Delta, SAS, Trans-Canada, Japan Air Lines and Swissair went for the DC-8. Continental, Western, TWA, Sabena, Air France, Air India and Lufthansa chose Boeing. By the time TWA picked the 707, on February 7, 1956, Boeing had an insurmountable lead. Even United Air Lines, which had given Douglas its biggest boost, eventually fell partly into the Boeing camp. Patterson decided that his company needed a smaller jet for some of its prime routes that did not require transcontinental range. Boeing promptly proposed a shortened, lighter version of the 707, called the 720. United ultimately purchased 28. (A joke of the day had it that Boeing possessed a Great Fuselage Machine that turned out one continuous fuselage from which the company cut off pieces as long as it wished.)

Beyond Boeing's eagerness to please, there actually was little to choose between the 707 and DC-8. Each plane had advantages and disadvantages. Passenger capacity for both was now about the same. Some pilots preferred the Big Eight's docility in the air; others liked the 707's greater speed and ruggedness. Still, Boeing had trounced Douglas in the battle for airlines' business. In 1959, it delivered seventy-three 707s, compared with Douglas' production of only 21 DC-8s.

Preferring to repeat earlier successes rather than to pioneer new technology, Douglas had focused too closely for too long on the DC-7. Perhaps the most devastating of Douglas' assumptions was to think that piston-craft could compete with jets. Boeing, by contrast, had been quick to move with the times and to adapt to the needs of its customers. And as its reward, for the first time ever, it had a successful commercial airliner to dispel the lingering taste of earlier failures.   ～～

The birth of the 707

In the 1950s aviation engineers were fond of observing wryly that all projects were governed by Murphy's First Law (if a component can fail, it will), not to mention Murphy's Second Law (if a device can possibly be hooked up backward, someone will do it that way). The Boeing designers and engineers charged with creating America's first jetliner, the 707, were determined that neither axiom would come into play when they set about developing a nearly fail-safe aircraft.

Boeing expended great effort and spent heavily in this quest for perfection. The team created 150 different designs before settling on the 707's configuration. Wind tunnel testing alone cost about a million dollars—including the investment of 25,000 man-hours just to build models for wind tunnel use. But the most important—and, at $15,000,000, the most expensive—development work took place in a specially walled-off area of a manufacturing building at Boeing's Renton, Washington, plant. There, Boeing took the unusual step—for the day—of constructing a prototype of the 707, first as a full-scale wooden mock-up, then as a flyable aircraft.

The prototype, known according to the company's internal numbering system as Model 367-80, or simply the Dash 80, was Boeing's chief means of overriding Murphy's Laws. Equipped with an array of oscillographs and automatic cameras that recorded every nuance of the plane's behavior under stress, it enabled Boeing engineers to test thoroughly and to refine all the 707's components and systems before production got under way. The result was a level of reliability astonishing for such a large aircraft.

Even after Boeing's assembly lines began turning out 707s by the score, the Dash 80's usefulness was not over. The prototype kept flying, testing modifications requested by different 707 customers and eventually serving as a test-bed for innovations employed in later designs, such as the 727. Some 20 years after work on it began in the secret assembly room, the Dash 80 was at last retired in 1972. It was turned over for safekeeping to the Smithsonian Institution, which pronounced it "one of the twelve most significant aircraft of all time."

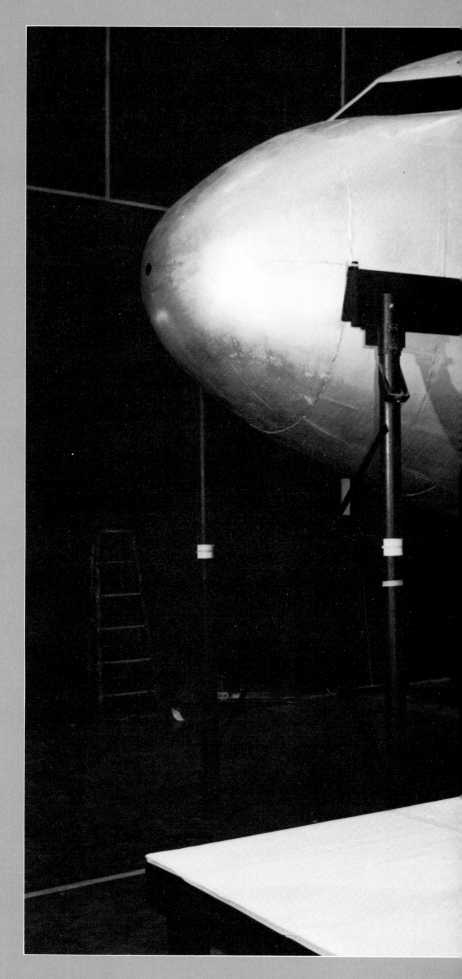

Two Boeing team leaders—mock-up and model supervisor Theodore Peck (left) and prototype project manager Lloyd Goodmanson (right)—study a model of the 707 prototype while another man tries the pilot's seat in a full-sized mock-up used to make sure that the aircraft's components would fit together properly.

A one-winged wooden mock-up of the prototype sits behind concealing partitions in the Renton factory. Since one wing would be a mirror image of

A dummy engine nacelle is fitted to the outboard pylon of the mock-up's wing.

The huge wooden wheels of the landing gear are measured for clearance.

the other, it was not necessary for the mock-up to have both.

In the plywood cockpit, engineers check out the placement of instruments.

The prototype's fuselage undergoes a pressurization test in February 1954. The rope nets were draped over the cargo doors to stop flying debris if internal pressure blew the doors out. The test was completed without incident.

Surrounded by scaffolding and file cabinets holding plans and specifications, the prototype awaits its engines in May of 1954, just two months shy of its roll-out. Engineers who were constantly solving problems presented by the plane's advanced design nicknamed the aircraft Tension Tech.

Inside a mock-up, technicians shift a dummy sofa as they work out a seating plan for the first-class lounge. The 707's passenger cabin was twice as large as that of Boeing's piston-engined Stratocruiser.

Workers on stepladders seal the inside of a "wet" wing—so called because it held fuel without the aid of internal tanks or bladders.

A specially designed roller squeezes the aluminum wing skin into shape.

Workers cut wire to fit and assemble it into bundles for later installation.

An electrician sorts some of the 62 miles of wire used in the plane.

A riveting machine pins together a leading-edge slat for the plane's wing.

At last in production after four years of testing the prototype, a gleaming 707 is rolled out to the paint hangar in Renton in March 1958.

The coin, the watch and the flower...

Within a few weeks you'll be able to board a luxurious Boeing 707. Your first flight in this jetliner will be one of the travel highlights of your life. You'll cruise serenely through high, weatherless skies, so completely free from vibration you'll be able to stand a half-dollar on edge. The 707 cabin, the most spacious aloft, will be so quiet you'll be able to hear the ticking of a watch. The flower you bought when you left will be fresh when you arrive, for the 600-mile-an-hour Boeing jet will carry you across a continent or an ocean in half the time needed by a conventional air-liner. Flight in the 707, even veteran airline travelers will find, is new and exciting—and secure. This superb luxury liner is by Boeing, the most experienced builder of multi-jet aircraft in the world.

These airlines already have ordered Boeing jetliners:

AIR FRANCE
AIR INDIA • AMERICAN
B.O.A.C. • BRANIFF • CONTINENTAL
CUBANA • LUFTHANSA
PAN AMERICAN • QANTAS • SABENA
SOUTH AFRICAN
TWA • UNITED • VARIG
Also MATS

BOEING 707 and 720

3
The race to catch up

We're buying airplanes with millions of dollars we don't have," said Collett E. Woolman, president of Delta Air Lines, just before his company ordered its first jetliners. "We're going to operate them off airports that are too small, in an air traffic control system that is too slow, and we must fill them with more passengers than we have ever carried before."

Woolman, one of the most respected of all airline executives, was no faintheart; he had expanded Delta from a tiny crop-dusting outfit in Louisiana to a powerfully competitive airline. He was merely expressing a deep-felt concern—shared by others—that the jets just might be ahead of their time.

Yet there was no turning back now. After the tragic false start provided by the Comet, the jet age had begun in earnest on Sunday, October 26, 1958, with the flight of Pan American World Airways *Clipper America* carrying 111 passengers from New York to Paris. The fact that most aviation historians herald that date as the birth of the jet age nettles the proud British. Not only did the 707 trail the ill-starred Comet 1 by nearly six and a half years, but 22 days before the Pan Am inaugural flight, a BOAC Comet 4, a successfully redesigned aircraft, had commenced North Atlantic jet service between London and New York. There was a vital difference between the aircraft, however; filled to capacity, the Comet 4 could carry only 67 passengers, scarcely more than half the number aboard Pan Am's 707.

Clipper America's 111 passengers—40 in first class and 71 in the coach section—represented the largest number of people ever to have boarded a scheduled flight, a sign of things to come. Indeed, Atlantic crossings by air already outnumbered those made by sea, and on domestic routes more and more people were taking advantage of low-cost tourist fares to fly instead of ride to their destination. The untapped market for the airlines was huge: Less than 10 per cent of the U.S. adult population had ever set foot on a scheduled airliner. With jets, said Eastern Air Lines president Eddie Rickenbacker, "air transportation should make more progress in the next ten years than we have been able to accomplish in the past 25."

Rickenbacker's blue sky prophecy was to prove correct—and then some. But if the new era of travel was truly to belong to the faster, bigger planes, major problems had to be solved. Airports, as Delta's Woolman had been quick to point out, were unprepared for the jets. Fuel storage

A Boeing advertisement from a 1958 Time sells the public on the 707's smooth, quiet, swift ride. Travelers quickly showed their enthusiasm for the new plane at the ticket counter: In the first three months of jet service, Pan American's 707s were filled to 90 per cent of capacity.

capacity had to be increased to supply the jets' huge tanks. Taxiways had to be widened, not to accommodate the planes' undercarriages but to save their engines, which hung so low that they could suck in debris from the ground on either side of the pavement. Runways were not long enough. Even the 9,500-foot strips at New York's Idlewild (today's John F. Kennedy International Airport) had to be extended so that jets bound for Europe could take off with a full load of fuel. Lengthening a runway cost roughly $1,000 per foot, and extensions ranging from 500 to more than 2,000 feet could put an almost unbearable financial burden on many airports and the cities they served. Congress would eventually come to the rescue in 1960 and allocate more than $57 million, matched dollar for dollar with local funds, for airport construction.

Fortunately for most airports, the jet age began slowly enough. Pan Am had the only six Boeings operating during the first three months after *Clipper America's* inaugural flight. (The rest of Pan Am's order for 20 of the first 707s was never filled; Trippe opted for a later model with longer range.) Until Boeing and Douglas could provide more jets, other lines would just have to wait—all, that is, except National Airlines. This tiny carrier was months away from receiving its first DC-8 when, on December 10, 1958, a 707, still bearing Pan Am markings but carrying National passengers, took off from New York for Miami, Florida.

That National could upstage American, United, TWA and Eastern was due entirely to its wily president, George Baker. A testy fellow, Baker had a long hate list of airline executives. At the top of that list was Eastern's Rickenbacker, with whom he was in direct competition on the lucrative New York-to-Miami route. To get the better of Rickenbacker, Baker turned to the man second on his list—Juan Trippe.

Baker knew that the delivery of Pan Am's jets coincided with the start of the line's annual winter doldrums, and he was sure Trippe would have trouble filling seats on his 707s before spring reinvigorated the business. Perhaps Baker could lease a couple of 707s from Pan Am in

Completing the first transatlantic commercial jet flight, a Comet 4 with 31 passengers aboard arrives at New York's Idlewild Airport on October 4, 1958. Although the Pan Am 707 behind the Comet also had just flown in from Europe, it had been on a test run and would not go into service until three weeks later.

the meantime and beat Eastern into the air with jets. To get them, he made Trippe an offer that sounded too good to be true—as indeed it was. In return for the use of two 707s for the 1958-1959 winter season, Baker proposed to pay a reasonable fee and to trade 400,000 shares of National's stock, plus an option to buy another 250,000 shares, for 400,000 shares of Pan Am. The deal would make Pan Am the major stockholder in National; by exercising the option, Pan Am could gain outright control. When Trippe signed the contract, it seemed that a long-standing dream of his was about to come true: At last he would possess domestic routes to feed passengers into his international flights.

Baker was no fool. He was sure that the Civil Aeronautics Board would disapprove the deal, but he gambled that the slow-moving CAB would not do so for several months to come. The delay would give him all winter to fly the two jets against Eastern's prop-driven Electras. And in the meantime National would receive the first of its own DC-8 fleet.

It happened just as Baker had planned. By the time the CAB reviewed his agreement with Trippe and disapproved it, National had turned a hefty profit flying Pan Am's 707s and enjoyed the distinction of being the first U.S. airline to offer domestic jet service.

Other airlines rushed to join the jet parade. American inaugurated its own service six weeks after National, with a 707 flight from New York to Los Angeles. Then late in March, Trans World Airlines flew its first 707 from San Francisco to New York. United, having ordered the Johnny-come-lately DC-8s, had to sit on the sidelines until September. During the intervening summer, rather than pit its piston-engined DC-7s in hopeless competition against TWA's and American's bigger, faster 707s, United temporarily abandoned nonstop transcontinental service—and a good thing it did, if Eastern's experience is an example of what the outcome might have been.

For all of Eddie Rickenbacker's optimism about jet travel's bright future, Eastern lagged far behind its competition in the acquisition of

Service equipment needed by a Pan Am 707, outlined on a runway, includes a maintenance boom in the rear and a fleet of trucks to supply fuel, water, food and cargo. The increased carrying capacity of the new jet created headaches for airports, not least of which was the processing of passengers' luggage.

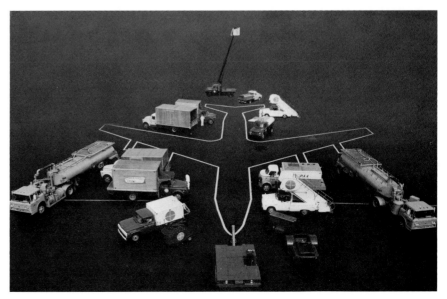

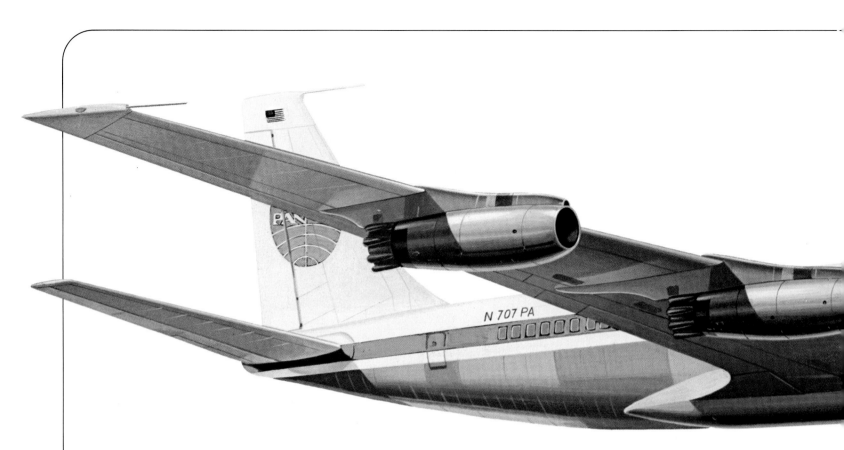

Pacesetter of the jet age

During a demonstration flight in 1957 aboard the prototype of the Boeing 707, American Airlines captain Sam Saint got his first taste of the jet age. "We burst out of the highest cloud layer into the upper air," he later recalled, "then it hit me. This was right—the way flying ought to be: smooth, solid, quiet and with obvious power to throw away. Everything about this machine built confidence."

That confidence was well placed, both for the airlines that would operate the 707 and for the company that risked building it at a time when other U.S. manufacturers were still insisting the future lay in propeller craft. With its four 13,000-pound-thrust turbojet engines, the 707 was 15 times more powerful, twice as fast and nearly double the size of the Boeing Stratocruiser, the largest commercial transport then in service.

The 707's capacious fuselage accommodated as many as 130 passengers. Its wings, designed to flex in rough air, were swept back 35 degrees and housed tanks holding 17,000 gallons of fuel, enough to give the plane nonstop transcontinental range. The engines were slung on pylons—a Boeing innovation—beneath the wings in a now-familiar arrangement that both enhanced the wings' lifting efficiency and contributed to easy engine maintenance.

From the start, Boeing's bold gamble paid off: The 707 quickly became the world's most widely used long-range airliner. By 1962, four years after their introduction, 707s had logged 1.7 million hours in the air and carried 30 million travelers 750 million passenger miles.

The 707's 145-foot-long fuselage, 130-foot wingspan and 257,000-pound weight made it the world's largest airliner when it appeared in 1958—and a cruising speed of 535 mph made it the fastest as well. This one, wearing Pan American World Airways' colors, inaugurated nonstop transatlantic jet Clipper service that same year.

jets. Rickenbacker had ordered DC-8s in time to be high up on the delivery schedule, but he had subsequently surrendered Eastern's place on the list to wait for a later model equipped with bigger engines. Delta Air Lines' president Woolman, holding a far lower priority for the DC-8, quickly grabbed Rickenbacker's abandoned order and beat Eastern into jet service by almost a year.

The effect was devastating. Eastern had been operating Electras between New York and Houston and filling an average of nine out of 10 seats on each flight. But after Delta launched DC-8 service on the same route, Eastern's traffic consisted largely of Delta's overflow. Two months later, Rickenbacker abandoned the once-lucrative New York-Houston nonstop routes, and he went on to take a beating in every other market where his prop planes were competing with jets.

Meanwhile, Continental Air Lines, the fourth domestic company to acquire jets, established 707 service on its Los Angeles-to-Chicago run, a market it had successfully penetrated during the piston era against the opposition of three well-established lines: United, American and TWA. Little Continental had been able to muscle in beside the titans because of the marketing acumen of its president, Robert Forman Six, whose stony mien, an associate once remarked, resembled a "fifth head on Mt. Rushmore." Something of an industry maverick, the formidable Six insisted—and had proved—that a small airline could compete with the giants if it demonstrated imagination and a gut feeling for passenger welfare. He thrived on playing David to the airline industry's Goliaths, meeting the competition with innovations that often stunned his more cautious rivals.

Continental had signed for only four 707s, but Six made the most of his modest investment. He had the planes' tails painted gold to symbolize a "Golden Jet" theme he thought up and specified plush interiors to make the competition's jets seem spartan. When passengers flocked to Continental, he accommodated them by flying his planes 16 hours a day, twice the other lines' average. He kept his schedules by handling maintenance late at night, when the aircraft were idle. And to avoid taking a jet out of service for a week to perform the overhaul required after 8,000 hours of operation, Continental's mechanics instituted "progressive maintenance." The overhaul was divided into tasks that could be completed during the regular nighttime maintenance shifts. Eventually, most airlines would adopt Continental's innovation.

Continental's success with its jet fleet was yet another goad to the airline industry to invest in the new planes. But the gamble was great: The planes cost $5,500,000 apiece, and what if these huge and complex machines turned out to be unsafe? A single crash would take 110 lives, nearly twice as many victims as would die in the fall of a DC-7. It took little imagination to see that a spate of accidents such as befell the Comet could scuttle the jet age and leave the airlines with scores of aircraft no one would fly on.

To reassure the public about the jets, the airlines placed only the most

With one engine and 28 feet of the starboard wing gone, Pan Am Flight 843 streams smoke and fire. A TWA flight engineer, Ernest Barter, photographed the burning jet from his automobile on San Francisco's Bayshore Freeway.

"Folks, we have a little minor problem"

Two minutes after taking off from San Francisco International Airport, bound for Hawaii on the 28th of June, 1965, Pan American Flight 843 was at 700 feet and climbing when suddenly the outboard engine on the Boeing 707's starboard wing burst into flames.

"All at once there was a big explosion and fire, and then the engine fell off," recalled one passenger, a teacher who had been sitting across the aisle from her children. "The fire kept getting larger and my children started to cry. I remember my daughter saying, 'Mommy, the fire is coming toward me.' Then the wing started to crumble and fall off."

In the cockpit Captain Charles Kimes could not see the damage so horrifyingly visible to the passengers, but he had felt the 707 shudder violently, then jerk to the right. Kimes wrestled with the controls, and by using the rudder and left aileron trim tab, he steadied the plane. For a moment he considered ditching in the Pacific but then decided to head for Travis Air Force Base 50 miles away.

With the jet now under marginal control and the fire subsiding, Kimes clicked on the microphone to talk to the anxious passengers. "Folks," he began, "we have a little minor problem. Well," he added, "maybe it's not so minor." Everybody burst out laughing, and Kimes kept up his chatter. A nurse on board the plane recalled later that passenger panic was "reduced immeasurably."

Unexpected hazards still lay ahead for Flight 843. As the plane neared Travis, Kimes found that the landing gear did not work; two crewmen had to crank the gear down by hand. Then, he spotted a dust devil, or small whirlwind, just off the end of the runway and swerved to avoid being caught in its turbulence. Finally, 19 harrowing minutes after the engine exploded, the captain brought the crippled jet—and its 152 grateful passengers—in for a perfect landing.

In an extraordinary photograph taken by passenger James Krick, flames eat away the 707's outer wing moments before the section broke off. Astonishingly, no one was injured by the hail of debris that fell on the busy San Francisco suburb below.

The demolished engine lies where it came to rest in an alley after crashing through the concrete wall of a cabinet shop and missing workmen by only 15 feet. The engine, subsequent analysis revealed, had exploded when a turbine wheel disintegrated.

At a news conference the day after the incident, Captain Charles Kimes modestly remarked that he had done "nothing outstanding." Boeing engineers felt otherwise. "We run just about every kind of test imaginable," said one technician, "but you never imagine a plane in this kind of situation remaining flyable. That cockpit was full of real pros."

Jagged pieces of metal protrude from the 707's charred wing. The fact that the fire advanced no farther along the wing with its fully loaded gas tanks was due to the quick response of the flight engineer, who cut off the fuel flow to the missing outboard engine.

seasoned pilots at the controls. As late as 1962, the average age of jetliner captains would be 50, compared with an average age of 38 for all airline pilots. A pilot switching from piston planes to jets had first to attend ground school to learn about the new aircraft. Then he spent several hours in a flight simulator that duplicated the controls and the feel of the plane before actually taking one aloft under the guidance of an instructor pilot. "The most important rule about a jet," said TWA Captain Harold Blackburn, "is that you must fly it by the book. If you try to fly it by the seat of the pants, you can be in a lot of trouble in a hurry."

But if jetliners were more demanding than pistons in this respect, they were less so in another. Because of the jet engine's simplicity, a 707 had at least 115 fewer instruments and controls for the engines than a Constellation. There were, for example, no carburetors on the turbojets and consequently no need for fuel-mixture controls. Having no propellers, a jet could dispense with the controls for de-icing them.

The planes, being new, had bugs that had to be worked out. Over a four-month period in 1959, the airlines reported more than 30 occasions on which the 707's hydraulically actuated landing gear refused to lower. Later, several DC-8s had similar troubles. In each case, the crew merely resorted to one of the jetliner's two back-up systems, one electrical and the other manual.

The difficulty was traced to the pump that supplied hydraulic fluid to the eight-wheel main gear. The pumps were wearing out faster than anyone had expected under the demands of daily airline operations and the temperature extremes they were exposed to—from 100° on the ground to 50° below zero at cruising altitude. Both Boeing and Douglas advised the airlines to modify the pumps, but while the corrective action was in progress, the embarrassing failures continued.

The undercarriage troubles were more vexing than dangerous, but there were other incidents—of the white-knuckle variety. Three months after Pan Am began jet Clipper service, one of the airline's new 707s was flying at night from Paris to New York at 35,000 feet. Captain W. Waldo Lynch, having left his copilot at the controls, stood in the cabin chatting with passengers when the autopilot disengaged and put the plane into a dive so shallow at first that the crew did not realize they were accelerating. As the seconds ticked by, the dive steepened, increasing the plane's speed until the aircraft began to buffet violently. Thrown to the cabin floor, Lynch, struggling against massive centrifugal forces created as the plane lapsed into a nose-down spiral, crawled along the aisle to the cockpit, where the copilot was battling to regain control of the craft. In front of him, the artificial horizon, an instrument that indicates whether an aircraft is flying level, was tumbling, and outside, the stars pinwheeled.

Somehow, Lynch managed to climb into his seat, and the navigator reached over to fasten his seat belt. "I have command," Lynch shouted and took a quick look at the altimeter. It was unwinding so fast that he could hardly read it. His feet seemed pinned to the floor and his arms felt weak, but with a superhuman effort he rolled the wings level. It took the combined efforts of both him and the copilot to end the dive. When the artificial horizon finally registered level flight, Lynch looked at the now-steady altimeter. It read 6,000 feet. They had plunged nearly 30,000 feet in less than a minute.

Lynch continued to Gander, Newfoundland, where he was scheduled for a refueling stop. Mechanics inspecting the plane found that the horizontal tail surfaces, wing panels and ailerons had been damaged. Pan Am dispatched another 707 to Gander to pick up the passengers while Lynch's craft underwent temporary repairs so that it could be flown to Seattle for further examination.

There, Boeing engineers discovered that in its 29,000-foot plunge, the 707 had approached the speed of sound at close to 700 miles per hour and had been subjected to stresses beyond those that Boeing thought the airplane could endure. If Lynch had not regained control when he did, the jet would have disappeared into the Atlantic, casting a dark shadow over the future of jet transportation.

Other pilots besides Lynch had harrowing experiences. Captain Howard Cone, taking a Pan American 707 on a practice flight over France, learned firsthand of the jets' built-in susceptibility to a phenomenon called the "Dutch Roll"—the tendency of a sweptwing aircraft under certain conditions to swing unchecked, like a wildly rocking hammock. The roll sometimes was induced by turbulence but also could occur during fairly steep turns and banks. The 707, with wings swept back five degrees more than the DC-8's, was more susceptible to this problem. Cone's 707 rocked so violently that an engine pod was wrenched from one of the wings, severing fuel and hydraulic lines. Cone managed to set the plane down safely in London. To remedy the problem, Boeing added three feet to the 707's vertical stabilizer, thus giving the pilot better control over the plane.

The 707 and DC-8 displayed another form of instability—they could stall in severe turbulence. The term for this was an "upset." Paul Soderlind, a flight operations executive at Northwest Orient Airlines, devised new techniques to combat it. He discovered that some pilots were slowing down in storms as a precaution against structural damage. In a jet, because the narrow, sweptback wings are less effective at low speeds than those of earlier airliners, throttling back could permit a severe downdraft or updraft to throw the plane into a stall. Recognizing the jets' superior structural strength, Soderlind recommended flying faster in storms to prevent stalls.

While the airlines and airplane manufacturers were working out the problems of the new planes, a new government regulatory body came into being in 1958, the Federal Aviation Agency, which replaced the old and tired Civil Aeronautics Administration. The first FAA Administrator was a former World War II fighter pilot and retired Air Force general named Elwood R. "Pete" Quesada. He was stocky, rosy-cheeked and he seemed to wear a perpetual smile. His appearance could not have

Braniff's flying colors

In the mid-1960s, as competition among airlines took a frenzied turn, Braniff International came up with what many considered an improbable scheme for sprucing up its image and attracting customers. It had its jet fleet painted in eye-catching colors: gaudy greens, blues and oranges. Within a year revenues had increased 18 per cent.

Encouraged by passenger response to its dazzling planes, Braniff in 1973 devised an even bolder plan for promoting its routes to "colorful and exciting" South America. It paid Alexander Calder, the American sculptor famous for his mobiles, $100,000 to create the world's first flying work of art (right).

Calder experimented with numerous designs, trying them out on six-foot-long models, before settling on a red, blue and yellow abstract pattern that was then transferred to a Braniff DC-8 by a team of painters. Free publicity from press coverage of Calder's masterwork more than repaid Braniff's investment.

A signed original, Flying Colors bears no Braniff logo, only the 13-foot-long name of artist Alexander Calder (inset).

been more deceptive. Quesada was trigger-tempered, demanding, forceful and determined to wipe out the old CAA's image of ineffective bureaucracy and weak-kneed leniency. Classic was the story of a CAA inspector who, when asked why he did not crack down on erring airline pilots, inquired plaintively, "How do you spank a Greek god?"

Quesada stamped his own commanding personality on the new agency. From the day he took office in the autumn of 1958, airlines and their crews, commercial and private pilots, and aircraft manufacturers received citations in unprecedented numbers for rule violations. Even while Pan Am's Waldo Lynch was being hailed as a hero for snatching his 707 from disaster, Quesada socked him with a $1,000 fine for being out of the cockpit unnecessarily and issued a stern edict: Henceforth, pilots would not be allowed to leave the flight deck for anything less than a call of nature. FAA inspectors riding the jets even began holding stop watches on captains when they went to the lavatory—six minutes was the unofficial time limit.

Yet Quesada was not relentlessly petty. One of his first acts was to begin modernizing the air traffic control system. At the time, air traffic

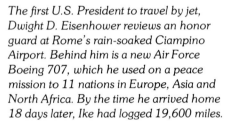

The first U.S. President to travel by jet, Dwight D. Eisenhower reviews an honor guard at Rome's rain-soaked Ciampino Airport. Behind him is a new Air Force Boeing 707, which he used on a peace mission to 11 nations in Europe, Asia and North Africa. By the time he arrived home 18 days later, Ike had logged 19,600 miles.

controllers were using outmoded radar inherited from the U.S. armed forces. The Air Force, however, was operating a much more advanced radar network as the eyes of its air defense system. And in April 1960 Quesada initiated research that would lead to the use of this equipment for the control of civilian aircraft. In the meantime, he began a landmark experiment with the FAA's antiquated equipment to track not only all the aircraft flying in airline corridors, but all planes flying at airline altitudes, between 24,000 and 35,000 feet. The test affected only 120,000 square miles of airspace in the Midwest, but it was the first step toward an air traffic control system that eventually would monitor every airliner from takeoff to landing.

Quesada's methods seemed arbitrary at times, and during his regime he feuded bitterly with every segment of civilian aviation from the Air Line Pilots Association to private flying clubs. Rightly or wrongly, Quesada regarded his job as a crusade to keep America's planes and airways safe for the flying public.

Public confidence in the jets was increased after the Air Force bought three 707s for its VIP transport fleet and assigned one of them to the President of the United States in 1959. The impetus for the switch from the piston-engined Constellation *Columbine* to a jet originated with Secretary of State John Foster Dulles. He had seen Soviet officials arrive at international meetings aboard the Tupolev 104 jet transport, a converted bomber that Aeroflot had been flying since 1956 *(pages 62-65),* and considered it degrading for Dwight Eisenhower not to avail himself of the most modern air transportation. He argued that if Air Force One were to be a 707, a bigger and better jet than the Russians', it would demonstrate America's technological superiority.

On August 26, 1959, Eisenhower jetted to Europe on a trip that took him to Germany, England, France and Scotland—more than 8,700 air miles covered in less than 20 hours' flying time. The President's jet enhanced his already considerable reputation as a globetrotter. In the piston-engined *Columbine,* he had averaged 120 hours of flying time a year, enough to carry him some 30,000 miles. But in 1960, his last year in office, the speed, quiet and comfort of the 707 induced him to spend 193 hours aloft, traveling almost 79,000 miles. But if Ike had quickly come to appreciate the world-shrinking virtues of the jet, so, it seems, had less illustrious travelers, both in America and abroad, and passengers were now flocking to the new planes in ever-increasing numbers.

Sheer novelty was a major incentive for one's first jet flight. It was something to brag about. "I just flew back from California in a jet" was more than a bald statement of fact; it was a badge of adventure. The airlines spent millions extolling the attractions of jet service but the best advertising was word of mouth. It was not exaggerating to say that no one who had experienced the vibration-free ride and the remarkable speed of a jet would ever be satisfied with a piston-engined plane again.

The question, What was it like? usually brought forth such prosaic adjectives as great, incredible or marvelous. But occasionally, a more vivid description could be found. After his first flight in a jet, Rod Serling, a prominent television writer, penned a letter to his brother: "I couldn't help but think as we flew over the midwestern plains and then the deserts and mountains how long it had taken our ancestors, less than a century ago, to travel a journey that was taking me less than six hours— and how far we had come in technology in so short a time. Nor have I ever felt so secure in an airplane. When we began our descent into Los Angeles, I had the sensation that we were riding an enormous railroad track toward the ground . . ."

If the experience of flying by jet produced any initial anxiety in the passenger, it was largely caused by unfamiliar sounds and new sensations. For several years, 707 and DC-8 captains would soothe nervous passengers with reassuring announcements—"That thumping sound you'll hear is merely our landing gear being lowered." Passengers accustomed to flying in piston-engined airliners had never heard the noise before; the wheel wells were in the engine nacelles, too far from the cabin for the undercarriage to be heard as it was raised or lowered. But in jets, the landing gear retracted directly into the fuselage.

Air travelers quickly discovered an unexpected bonus in flying by jet—a general and marked decrease in airsickness, attributed almost entirely to the steadiness of flight at altitudes where plane-tossing turbulence was rarely encountered. But many passengers traded a queasy stomach for a troublesome new disorientation, jet lag, the inability of the body to adjust quickly to a distant time zone. Jet trips disrupted biological rhythms. It was only too easy to leave New York for Los Angeles at 5 p.m., arrive as early as 8 local time and then stay awake until midnight; by then, of course, it was 3 a.m. in New York. Fatigue, insomnia and constipation—all symptoms of jet lag—became prevalent. Moreover,

2. Flying between beacons ABC and DEF, the pilot selects a course—in this case 180 degrees from station DEF—and holds it by keeping the course deviation indicator (CDI) needle centered. Here, the needle is deflected to the left, telling the pilot to turn left to remain on course; the "to" in the window shows that the course is toward the station.

VOR RECEIVER/CDI

180

TO

CONE OF SILENCE

VOR STATION ABC

Tracking an unseen pathway in the sky

To find their way from one airport to another and land safely even in inclement weather, airline pilots have a variety of sophisticated radio aids at their disposal, as shown in this series of diagrammatic renderings.

For cross-country navigation, VOR, or very high frequency omnidirectional range, radio beacons transmit continuous signals that can be picked up by the airliner's VOR receiver and displayed to the pilot on a cockpit instrument known as the course deviation indicator (CDI). The readings of the CDI needle are independent of the aircraft's magnetic compass heading and show where the course is in relation to the airplane. Small windows on the instrument's face tell which course has been set and whether it is toward or away from the VOR station.

On arriving at the destination, the pilot

relies on an instrument landing system (ILS) that helps to guide the plane onto the runway. The ILS consists of a localizer beacon that tracks the aircraft onto the runway centerline and a glide slope transmitter whose beams are angled about three degrees from the horizontal to bring the plane down at a steady rate of descent.

These signals are picked up by the plane and displayed by the glide slope (GS) and localizer needles (LOC) on the ILS receiver. Another instrument, the marker beacon receiver, picks up signals from the two marker beacons along the approach path that tell the pilot the distance to the runway threshold. At the second beacon, an approach lighting system helps the pilot to judge visually the last few thousand feet before touchdown.

VOR STATION DEF

MARKER BEACON RECEIVER

O M

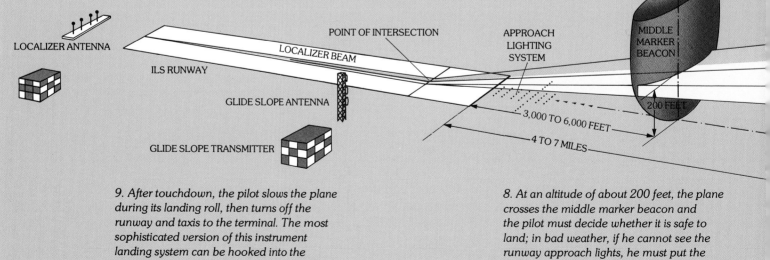

LOCALIZER ANTENNA

POINT OF INTERSECTION

APPROACH LIGHTING SYSTEM

MIDDLE MARKER BEACON

LOCALIZER BEAM

ILS RUNWAY

GLIDE SLOPE ANTENNA

GLIDE SLOPE TRANSMITTER

200 FEET

3,000 TO 6,000 FEET

4 TO 7 MILES

9. After touchdown, the pilot slows the plane during its landing roll, then turns off the runway and taxis to the terminal. The most sophisticated version of this instrument landing system can be hooked into the aircraft's automatic pilot and programed to land the plane in absolute zero-zero weather.

8. At an altitude of about 200 feet, the plane crosses the middle marker beacon and the pilot must decide whether it is safe to land; in bad weather, if he cannot see the runway approach lights, he must put the airplane into a climb and either make a new approach or fly to another airport.

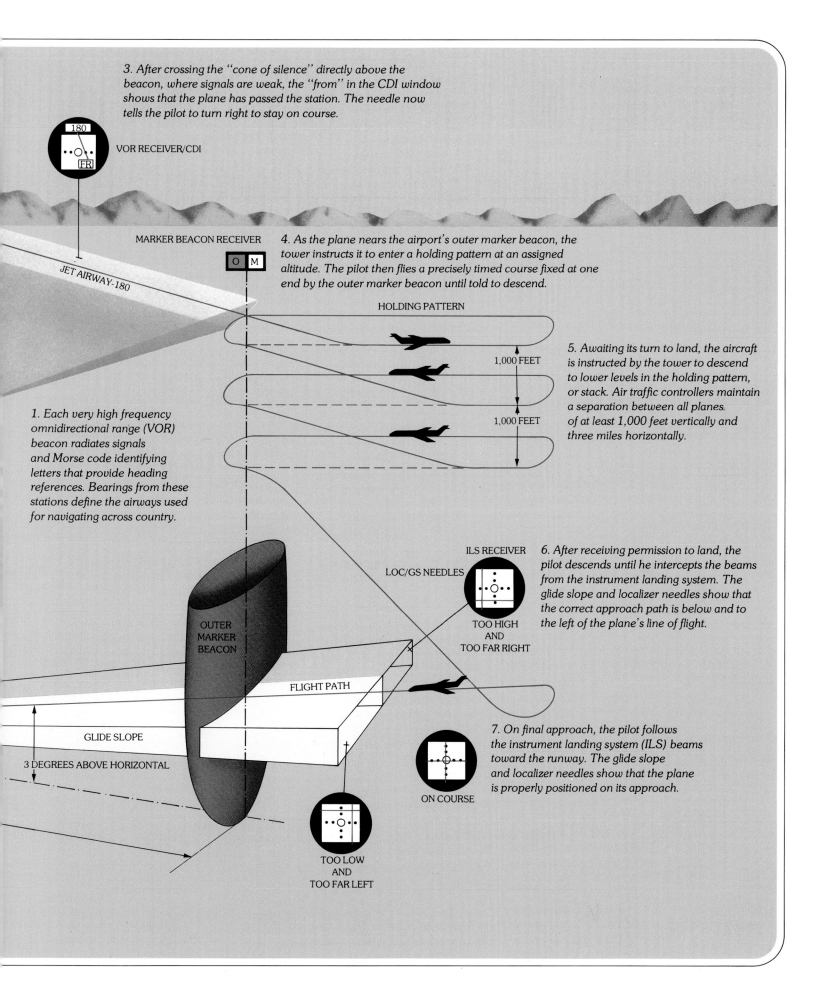

3. After crossing the "cone of silence" directly above the beacon, where signals are weak, the "from" in the CDI window shows that the plane has passed the station. The needle now tells the pilot to turn right to stay on course.

VOR RECEIVER/CDI

MARKER BEACON RECEIVER

JET AIRWAY-180

O M

4. As the plane nears the airport's outer marker beacon, the tower instructs it to enter a holding pattern at an assigned altitude. The pilot then flies a precisely timed course fixed at one end by the outer marker beacon until told to descend.

HOLDING PATTERN

1,000 FEET

1,000 FEET

5. Awaiting its turn to land, the aircraft is instructed by the tower to descend to lower levels in the holding pattern, or stack. Air traffic controllers maintain a separation between all planes of at least 1,000 feet vertically and three miles horizontally.

1. Each very high frequency omnidirectional range (VOR) beacon radiates signals and Morse code identifying letters that provide heading references. Bearings from these stations define the airways used for navigating across country.

ILS RECEIVER

LOC/GS NEEDLES

TOO HIGH
AND
TOO FAR RIGHT

6. After receiving permission to land, the pilot descends until he intercepts the beams from the instrument landing system. The glide slope and localizer needles show that the correct approach path is below and to the left of the plane's line of flight.

OUTER
MARKER
BEACON

FLIGHT PATH

GLIDE SLOPE

3 DEGREES ABOVE HORIZONTAL

ON COURSE

7. On final approach, the pilot follows the instrument landing system (ILS) beams toward the runway. The glide slope and localizer needles show that the plane is properly positioned on its approach.

TOO LOW
AND
TOO FAR LEFT

jet lag could impair judgment to such a degree that some firms ordered traveling executives not to decide policy or sign contracts within 24 hours of a five-hour time change. At least one airline instructed its air crews not to reset their watches for the time at their destination—and to eat and sleep in accordance with their back-home schedules.

Nevertheless, travelers loved the jets—and so did the airlines. The turbojets' reliability, something the industry measured with Time Between Overhauls, or TBO, delighted executives. The best piston engine had a TBO of about 800 hours, and initially the FAA extended that interval to 1,000 hours for the jets. By 1962, the average TBO had risen to 4,000 hours, and eventually the FAA would discard all TBO schedules, provided that a few critical components were inspected or replaced at specified intervals. This represented an enormous saving in money. The complete overhaul of an engine required the disassembly of all major parts at a cost of $90,000; in the past airlines had paid only $114,000 for a complete DC-3, fresh from the Douglas factory.

The jets' fleetness and spacious interiors were cause for joy, too. The difference in speed between the fastest piston-engined transport and a jet was 240 miles an hour, a differential almost as great as all the speed increases made by commercial airplanes between 1918 and 1953. In those 35 years, transports had struggled from a top speed of 90 miles an hour in 1918 to 350 miles an hour in 1953; the jets cruised at 590 miles an hour and could carry twice as many passengers as the DC-7s. These two advantages made it possible for an airline to fly a specified number of passenger miles with fewer jets than with piston-engined aircraft and helped to offset the high cost of the new planes.

Fuel consumption remained heavy, but even here there was cause for celebration. Fully loaded, a 707 or DC-8 had a fuel efficiency of about 42 passenger miles per gallon, while a DC-7 could deliver 59 passenger miles with the same quantity of fuel. But these figures were moderated by the low price of the kerosene used in jets—10 cents per gallon in the early 1960s compared with 25 cents a gallon for the high-octane fuel that powered piston engines. In fact, the overall cost per passenger mile of the 707 and DC-8 turned out to be lower than that of a DC-7. The introduction of turbofan engines in 1960 cut fuel consumption, lowering costs further. And there was an additional boon: They were less noisy than the turbojet.

Noise had been one of the negative side effects of the jet age. People living near airports complained about a whole range of discordant sounds, from the banshee wail of taxiing jets to the ceiling-shaking thunder of the engines on takeoff. Not too long after jets began serving Dallas, residents of a big apartment building painted a huge sign on the roof, "JETS GO HOME!" That protest was to be multiplied a thousand times. To counter it, early 707s and DC-8s were equipped with a cluster of "pipe organ" tubes at the rear of each engine. These diffused the jets' noise to some extent. Unhappily, they also reduced thrust by as much as 10 per cent and added about $10,000 a month to each plane's fuel costs. Now the turbofan engine offered a solution. The roar of a jet is caused primarily by the high speed of the exhaust from the combustion chambers. Diluting the exhaust with slower air passed around the engine by the fan makes the turbofan noticeably quieter than the turbojet *(page 23)*.

The advantages of the jets were appreciated by airlines the world over. Of the first two hundred 707s and DC-8s ordered, more than half were exported. Along with the aircraft they bought from American companies, some European and Asian airlines purchased American technical know-how to help launch them into the jet age. United Air Lines' highly regarded training facilities in Denver became an aeronautical United Nations, teaching foreign pilots how to fly jets. West Germany's Lufthansa continued to owe much of its success to a technical mission from Trans World Airlines. When Lufthansa started up again after World War II, TWA coached the German airline in every phase of its operations, from marketing to flying. By the time Lufthansa ordered jets, it had been thoroughly trained in American airline methods.

For many nations a jet-equipped airline became a symbol of prestige, a means of showing the flag. Often heavily subsidized by their governments, such airlines posed what independent U.S. airlines regarded as an unfair threat. By 1962, Pan Am found itself competing with 13 airlines crossing the Pacific, 23 in Central and South America, and 29 over the North Atlantic.

Competition among world airlines for passengers became increasingly intense. And nowhere was the contest more apparent than among those flying the Atlantic. Airlines never seriously tried to rival steamship companies in luxury; there was a limit to the comfort that could be designed into a relatively narrow cylindrical tube holding more than 100 seats. Still, first-class passengers were coddled with such amenities as free lounging slippers and three choices of entrée for dinner along with as much alcohol as they could drink. In 1961, TWA introduced first-run movies for first-class passengers. This sales device proved so successful that other airlines scrambled to install projectors in their planes as soon as TWA's exclusive contract with the movie supplier expired.

Despite their jet-age rivalries, the world's airlines learned to cooperate with one another. Half a dozen major companies created a spare parts pool in the early 1960s that, according to one member, Air France, slashed inventory costs by 70 per cent. The men in the cockpit in turn banded together in the International Federation of Air Line Pilots, an organization dedicated to the principle of learning from one anothers' experiences. Thus no incident concerning safety in the sky could be swept under the rug of national pride.

The jet shrank the world and, through travel and commerce, brought peoples together. Destinations a week away by automobile or bus, or four days by train, suddenly were reachable in a few hours. Pittsburgh was next door to Paris, and Louisville around the corner from London. Suddenly everyone could be a jet setter. ∾

A cartoon from a 1965 issue of Life depicts the sybaritic pleasures of jet travel. In the mid-1960s, when airline competition heated up, TWA was first to offer movies, luring customers with the line, "Don't just sit there! Fly TWA and see a movie on the way." The result: six to eight more passengers per flight.

4

A clash of titans

During the 1950s, while Great Britain and the United States were struggling for supremacy in the jet field, France was quietly working to carve out its own share of the fabulous new market. Noting that de Havilland, Boeing and Douglas had decided to build long-range aircraft, the French government in the autumn of 1951 sponsored a competition among the country's aircraft builders for the design of a short- to medium-range jetliner that could carry about 60 passengers up to 1,200 miles. Such an aircraft would be ideally suited to the short distances between European cities that the bigger jets could not fly economically and might recapture the prominence that French aviation had enjoyed at the end of World War I.

Soon, engineers at six companies were hard at work drafting entries for the competition. In September 1952, France's civil aviation agency announced the winner—Sud Aviation, a plane manufacturer in Toulouse that had come up with a most unusual scheme for placing the jet's two engines at the tail, rather than on the wings. Sud Aviation named its entry Caravelle, after the small sailing ships that were workhorses of commerce and exploration in the 15th and 16th Centuries.

The new plane had its critics. The naysayers worried that an aft-engined airliner would be tail-heavy and dangerous to fly. They also doubted the wisdom of powering a jetliner roughly the size of a DC-6 with only two engines: If one failed on takeoff or landing, would there be enough power to keep the Caravelle airborne? Finally, they questioned the entire concept of a jet built for hops of only a few hundred miles. Flying from one city to the next, the Caravelle—or so the argument went—would have too little cruising time at the high altitudes where the fuel-gulping jet engine is most efficient.

Fortunately the critics did not prevail. In seven years of development and testing, the Caravelle proved all fears unfounded. So that the Caravelle could fly safely if an engine failed, the designers installed powerful Rolls-Royce Avon turbojets, each developing 12,600 pounds of thrust, equivalent in power to six of the piston engines on DC-6s. And because the Caravelle had only two engines, it made a profit for airlines on flights as short as 200 miles. Since the engines were at the rear, the wings were uncluttered, giving the plane exceptional maneuverability—and there was little cabin noise. Indeed, it was so quiet inside a Caravelle that passengers would show a preference for the plane over turboprop airliners. And not least of the Caravelle's qualities was its

Six Boeing 727 jets of the many-hued Braniff fleet snug up to loading bridges at Dallas-Fort Worth Airport in 1979. The 727's 2,000-mile range, roomy passenger cabin and ability to take off on less than 5,000 feet of runway helped make the plane the world's best-selling airliner; more than 1,600 were in operation by the early 1980s.

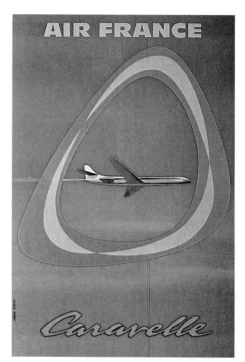

A passenger aboard a French-built Caravelle jet (left) basks dreamily in sunlight streaming through one of the triangular windows that were celebrated in an Air France poster (above). The unusual shape provided as wide a downward view as a rectangular window but was more resistant to stress.

beauty. "It was," one airline captain said, "the only airplane I ever flew that just had to be called 'She.'"

Air France, naturally, was first in line for the Caravelle. Its order for a dozen of the new airliners in November 1955 galvanized the British into action. They suddenly realized that British European Airways, which flew many of the same routes on the Continent as Air France, would have to replace its turboprops with short-haul jets or face economic defeat at the hands of the French.

But for a British airline to fly a French jet was unthinkable; Britain must build its own small jetliner, and BEA already knew what it wanted: a plane that could lift a 19,000-pound payload from a 6,000-foot runway and carry it 1,000 miles. In addition, the cabin had to be 11 feet across, wide enough to seat three passengers on each side of the aisle.

At BEA's urging, three companies entered a competition to build the new jet, and on paper at least, all three satisfied the airline's specifications. But one company had an unbeatable edge—the proud de Havilland concern. Everyone knew that de Havilland had the most experience with jets.

There was, however, a problem: Before work could actually begin on the plane, the government had to grant approval. BEA was, after all, a government-owned airline, and all equipment purchases required a nod from the Air Ministry. But at the moment, the Air Ministry took a dim view of the country's aircraft industry; it saw a field overcrowded with small, inefficient, unprofitable companies that could not compete with the American giants Boeing and Douglas. Its solution was to tie approval of the plane, known as the D.H.121, to a merger of de Havilland, Hawker Siddeley and Bristol, the three manufacturers that had submitted designs to the Air Ministry. The companies balked, refusing this kind of "shotgun wedding," as one British aviation journal put it. Faced with BEA's determination to have the D.H.121 or nothing and the aircraft manufacturers' intransigence, the Ministry relented and reluctantly accepted a consortium of builders that would allow de Havilland, Hawker Siddeley and Bristol to retain their individual identities. It was something of a pyrrhic victory for de Havilland, however. In 1960, the company was bought by Hawker Siddeley and in the takeover the D.H.121 was renamed the Trident.

The design for the Trident called for engines in the rear like the Caravelle, which was now in service with several airlines. But instead of two, there was to be a third, mounted inside the fuselage, behind the cabin. Air for this engine would come from an intake just in front of the horizontal stabilizers. Recognizing how much power three Rolls-Royce turbojets would provide, Hawker Siddeley began to make the plane bigger and heavier. At its largest the Trident would have been capable of carrying 12 tons of passengers and cargo as far as 2,070 miles. But BEA would not be swayed from its original specifications and insisted that the Trident be scaled down. If it was not, the airline would cancel its order. Hawker Siddeley complied, concentrating on a plane with a 79-passenger capacity and 1,000-mile range.

The Trident would be unconventional in more than its engine con-

A foreshortened view of the Trident, Britain's answer to France's Caravelle, shows the T tail, with the third engine buried in it. The Hawker Siddeley jetliner was the first commercial aircraft to use electronic gear enabling it to make an automatic touchdown in bad weather.

figuration. The horizontal tail stabilizers were to be mounted on top of the vertical stabilizer, an arrangement known as a T tail that made the plane exceptionally stable at low speeds. So that the Trident could operate fully loaded from a 6,000-foot runway, special wing flaps were developed that provided more lift on takeoff. And in yet another innovation the nose gear was to be installed off-center, allowing it to be retracted to the side instead of forward or to the rear; this made room for baggage near the front of the plane, helping balance the weight of the engines at the tail.

Across the Atlantic, just about the time that BEA came up with its specifications for the D.H.121, or Trident, a young engineer at Boeing, Jack Steiner, was made assistant chief of the Preliminary Design Unit. Fresh from the bustling, well-established 707 program, Steiner entered an uncharted wilderness of tenuous theories and vague goals. His chief task was to inspect and appraise a thick file of proposals for a short- to medium-range jet transport that could fly in and out of airports too small for the 707. The dossier contained no fewer than 38 different designs.

Boeing, at that point, was of two minds about building a smaller jet. The field was already crowded with competitors, not only abroad, but at

The Dash 80, the 707 prototype, flies fitted with a fifth jet to analyze the effects of an aft-mounted engine. The ungainly exhaust pipe diverted the extremely hot jet blast to prevent damage to the tail.

home as well. Douglas had a team working on a scaled-down version of the DC-8, and Convair, with orders from TWA and Delta on the books, had begun building the 880, a four-engined jetliner about two thirds the size of the 707 and intended for medium-length routes in the 500- to 1,000-mile range.

A number of executives at Boeing wondered if a short-haul jet would be worth the effort. Boeing already had the 720, the lighter and slightly truncated version of the 707 built originally for United Air Lines. Would not the production of a smaller jet draw sales away from the 720? The doubters seemed vindicated when the airlines began showing a preference for the 720 over Convair's 880, even though the two planes were similar in size. Steiner, however, remained convinced of the need for a brand-new jet transport, one that could match the 707 for economy, yet serve airports with short runways. If such a plane could be built, it would not undercut the 720, he reasoned—but it would effectively shut out the turboprops like the Lockheed Electra and the British Vickers Viscount.

Boeing spent a full year on preliminary studies before naming Steiner, in May 1957, head of an official task force, to settle on the design of such an aircraft. Right from the start, Steiner's team faced formidable problems. For one thing, the airlines could not agree on the kind of aircraft they needed. United wanted a small jet but insisted that four engines were absolutely essential for the airline's lucrative operations in mile-high Denver, where the relatively thin atmosphere required increased power for takeoff. (Douglas had drawn up a plane, to be called the DC-9, that satisfied United, but the idea was scrapped when no other airline expressed interest.) Eastern believed a four-engined plane would cost too much to operate; it preferred two power plants but might settle for a third as added security on its overwater routes to the Caribbean. Eastern also warned that it would reject an airliner that could not operate from short-runway airports such as New York's La Guardia. TWA's engineers leaned toward three engines as both safer than two and more economical than four.

Evaluating the airlines' various needs, Boeing settled on a three-engined model. But where should these power plants be placed? Steiner's crew wrestled with several concepts. It even contemplated mounting the third engine on one side of the fuselage, with the other two tucked under the wings. Surprisingly, this arrangement worked aerodynamically, but the idea was discarded on the ground that passengers would reject a plane that looked lopsided. Boeing finally borrowed the scheme worked out for the Trident—positioning the third engine behind the cabin—and adopted the Trident's T tail as well.

Technical problems were by no means the only ones Steiner's group had to work out. Boeing's marketing experts had told Steiner to come up with a jet that would sell for no more than three million dollars, about the price of a Caravelle. But this would severely restrict its dimensions and limit the number of passengers to 75—

too few in Steiner's opinion. Moreover, a smaller plane would not yield the low passenger-mile costs that Boeing and the airlines were after. But if Steiner added more seats, the bigger craft would be less likely to meet either Eastern's short-runway requirements or Boeing's own price ceiling. And even if Boeing were somehow to build a jet for three million dollars, it would be virtually identical, from the airlines' point of view, to the Caravelle and Trident.

For a while it seemed wiser for the company to abandon the project and join forces with the British or French in selling—and perhaps even building—the Trident or the Caravelle in the United States. But the idea, though seriously considered, never got beyond the talking stage—and just as well. For gradually the Steiner team, which had gone on working, had brought within grasp a jetliner that promised to surpass all competition.

In the two years of the task force's existence, the number of design studies had grown from 38 to 150. Of these, 68 had undergone wind tunnel evaluation before the team, which now consisted of 1,000 engineers, made its final choice. Designated the 727, the plane would embody three features that would make it a truly remarkable aircraft while at the same time meeting the diverse requirements of the airlines.

First, the 727's fuselage would be the same width as that of the 707/720 series. This would not only cut tooling costs for Boeing and maintenance costs for the airlines, but it would allow six-abreast seating of 120 passengers. Second, the engine chosen for the 727 promised unheard-of economies. Boeing had all but signed a contract for a Rolls-Royce turbofan when the Pratt & Whitney Aircraft Company showed Steiner the blueprint for a new turbofan, the JT8D. Though the concept had been worked out in less than a week under the pressure of the approaching deal between Boeing and Rolls-Royce, the Pratt & Whitney engine looked so good Boeing could not easily pass it up. Forty per cent of its thrust would come from a large fan in front *(page 23),* making it much more economical to run than any other engine of the day, and much quieter as well. Moreover, in selecting the JT8D, Boeing met United Air Lines' demand for a plane with power; the three engines, each developing 15,000 pounds of thrust, could easily lift a fully loaded 727 from Denver's mile-high runways.

The third feature of the 727 was a unique arrangement of wing flaps. In the space of just a few seconds the wing's normal blade-like shape, ideal for high-speed flight, could be modified into a kind of "parasol" *(page 110)* for landings. ("On this bird," one captain would later remark admiringly, "you don't lower the flaps. You disassemble the whole damned wing.") When fully opened, the flaps increased the 727's wing area by 25 per cent, permitting the plane virtually to float to the ground. This was exactly what Eastern needed; so equipped, the 727 could take off from and land on short runways, such as the 4,980-foot strip at New York's La Guardia.

As a jet engine is hoisted toward them, Boeing workers prepare to connect it to a 727 fuselage. Designers standardized the 727 so that 90 per cent of the parts were identical in every variation of the plane.

But if Steiner's fledgling airliner incorporated these three expensive features, it would have to sell for $4.2 million—a third more than Boeing's marketing experts had stipulated. In the autumn of 1960, the board of directors put the decision of whether to go ahead in the hands of president Bill Allen. Daunted by the $100 million estimated development costs, Allen announced that Boeing would proceed only if the company received firm orders for at least one hundred 727s by December 1. But with the deadline just a day away, it found it had only 20 orders from United, with options for another 20 of the aircraft, and 40 from Eastern. The total, including the 20 options, was 20 short of Allen's 100-aircraft goal. Allen faced a dilemma. If he did not proceed with the 727, Boeing would lose millions that it had already spent bringing the design this far and would have to lay off hundreds of workers. If the company went ahead, it would have to sell nearly a billion dollars' worth of the planes before seeing a profit. A decision had to be made. Allen, swayed in the end by Steiner's conviction that the 727 was a winner, took a deep breath and authorized start-up.

The first 727 rolled out of the factory two years later, on November 27, 1962, and went almost immediately into flight tests that showed it to be an even finer aircraft than Steiner or anyone else had dreamed, with

A bird of a different feather

The most challenging problem confronting the designers of the Boeing 727 was what kind of wing to give their new bird: The requirements were for an airfoil that would enable the transport to cruise at nearly 600 mph, yet take off and land on relatively short runways. Boeing's designers spent 5,000 hours testing various configurations in wind tunnels, and the result was a compound wing loaded with "feathers," or sophisticated aerodynamic devices. When extended, slats and flaps on the edges of the wing curved downward, allowing the jet to descend slowly to earth. During high-speed hops between cities, the slats and flaps retracted to create a sweptback, streamlined blade. Marveled one pilot: "It's a magic carpet wing."

A Boeing 727 has its flaps and slats fully extended in the landing position.

A cross section of the 727 wing shows the shape that the wing assumes for most flight regimes. The leading-edge slats and triple-slotted trailing-edge flaps retract to form a compact, uninterrupted surface that has low drag characteristics.

When the slats and the three-part flaps are extended, they provide a large area on top of the wing, producing the lift needed for slow approaches to short runways. The openings behind the slats and between the flap segments also boost lift by keeping the airflow smooth and close to the wing.

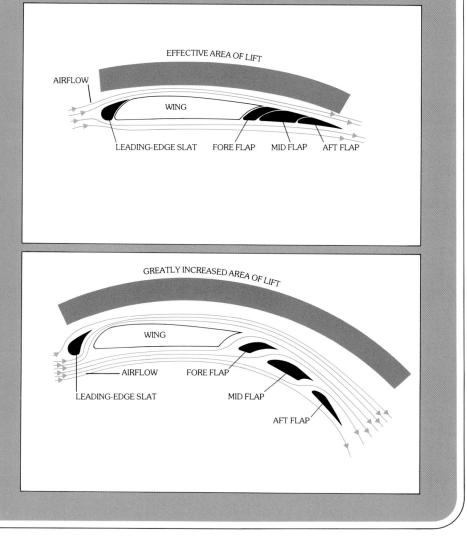

110

an amazing capacity for taking off from, and landing on, short runways at a steep angle of ascent or descent. A veteran aviation writer wangled a ride on one test flight that was to simulate an engine failure on takeoff from a high-altitude airport—Butte, Montana. As the jet accelerated down the runway, the writer—who was sitting in the cockpit jump seat—looked apprehensively at the Rocky Mountains towering just three miles ahead. Halfway down the 6,800-foot strip, the copilot reduced thrust on the right engine to idle. The startled writer gulped, but the 727 took it all in stride. The pilot pointed its nose into the air, and the plane climbed swiftly on two engines over the mountains. "Quite a machine," the test pilot said. "I had the feeling," the writer reported later, "that he would have enjoyed getting out and patting the 727 affectionately on her metal hide."

Besides exhibiting astonishing takeoff performance, the 727 was an admirable 15 knots faster than wind tunnel tests had predicted. Equally amazing, fuel consumption was 10 per cent less and payload 10 per cent greater than Boeing had expected. All in all, the 727 added up to a jetliner well worth its $4.2 million price tag, and Boeing mapped out a nationwide tour for the fourth 727 off the assembly line to stimulate sales. The road show got rave reviews not only from airline officials but from the press. Takeoffs could be alarming for the uninitiated, as the plane pitched its nose upward 18 degrees before the main landing gear left the ground. "No one was prepared for that steep ascent," said a reporter who had gone for a demonstration ride. "Practically everyone aboard thought that the tail was dragging and that we'd never get airborne."

In a further sales effort, Boeing showed off the plane to the world on a trip that took it to Europe, South Africa, the Middle East, India, Australia and Japan. On one Australian demonstration flight, the pilot brought the plane to a complete stop only 1,500 feet from touchdown, to the applause of the entire cabin. The short landing was possible because of the 727's powerful brakes as well as its low approach and landing speed. "I must stress," wrote a British flier, "the visible, palpable effect of that slow approach speed. It gives the pilot time when he needs it most—when the chips are down, in low ceilings and poor visibility."

The 727 soon became known as a superb airliner and began to sell briskly. The initial United and Eastern orders were followed by a flood of contracts from both foreign and U.S. airlines. Boeing's billion-dollar gamble was paying off.

Not since the legendary DC-3 had any transport received such pilot trust and affection as the 727. Among its crews the 727 quickly acquired a reputation as a pilot's airplane, a craft that handled quickly and easily, more like a fighter, in fact, than a heavy transport. But 19 months after the first trijet went into service, there occurred the first of a series of tragedies that reminded pilots of what some of them seemed to have forgotten: For all its superb qualities, the 727 had to be flown by the book just like the 707 and DC-8.

On August 16, 1965, a United Air Lines 727, Flight 389 from La Guardia, was approaching Chicago's O'Hare Airport across Lake Michigan. The pilot acknowledged clearance to descend from 14,000 to 6,000 feet. But instead of leveling off at the new altitude, the plane flew into the water and exploded. All aboard were killed.

Why United's Flight 389 plunged into Lake Michigan remains a mystery to this day. Investigators could recover only part of the wreckage, and the flight recorder, which might have solved the puzzle, was never found. Circumstantial evidence suggested that in the final minutes the 727 was descending too fast. The wreckage indicated that the pilot had leveled off, but too late to avoid crashing. Perhaps the crew had misread the altimeter.

Less than three months later, an American Airlines 727 plowed into a hill while on final approach to Cincinnati airport in poor weather. One of the survivors, an off-duty captain with the airline, told investigators that the initial descent seemed rapid, and the flight recorder confirmed this impression. The sink rate was recorded at 2,100 feet per minute; the recommended maximum at low altitude was about 800 feet per minute. The official verdict on the accident was that the crew had failed to monitor instruments properly. By the time they realized their predicament, it was too late to slow their descent, and the plane crashed short of the runway.

On November 11, 1965, only three days after the Cincinnati accident, a United 727 approaching Salt Lake City radioed from 10,000 feet: "We have the runway in sight." The copilot, who was flying the ship, began to descend quickly, at more than 2,000 feet per minute over the last 90 seconds of the flight and 2,300 feet per minute during the final 60 seconds, nearly three times the maximum recommended by United. The only way to check such a rate with wing flaps fully extended is to speed up and increase lift. When the jet was 90 seconds from touchdown, the copilot reached for the throttles. "Not yet," the captain said. Those two words doomed the flight. By the time the captain took over the controls and shoved the throttles forward seven seconds from the runway, nothing could have been done to save the plane. The 727's undercarriage hit the ground more than 100 yards short of the runway and collapsed. The jet caught fire and slid on its torn belly for some 3,000 feet, flames enveloping the cabin. Of the 85 passengers aboard, 41 perished.

When the fourth crash—this one of a Japanese 727 attempting to land at Tokyo International Airport—came nearly three months later, members of Congress demanded that the trijet be grounded. But the Civil Aeronautics Board, unconvinced that the plane was at fault, resisted the pressure and established a special committee that, after a thorough investigation of the 727's flight characteristics, exonerated the airliner. The cause of the accidents lay not so much with the 727 as with

Bill Lear and his Cadillacs of the air

In 1959, while the large aviation companies were concentrating on developing short- to medium-range jetliners, William P. Lear—an electronics genius with only an eighth-grade education—was obsessed with one thought: He would build a small jet for businessmen's use.

As the inventor of the first lightweight autopilot for military jets and other electronic devices, Lear already had three decades of aviation experience when, in 1962, he sold his $100 million electronics firm and risked $11 million on the first twin-engined Learjet. Just nine months later, Lear's Model 23 took to the air.

By June 1965, twenty-six of the small, rather cramped planes had been sold for $600,000 each, and that year the Learjet set three world speed records for its class by flying from Los Angeles to New York and back in 10 hours and 21 minutes. Models 24 and 25, with several major improvements, rolled out to great acclaim in 1966. Customers loved the little jets, apparently agreeing with Lear that "you can't stand up in a Cadillac either." But by early 1967 inadequate marketing techniques and unprofitable subsidiaries forced Lear to sell his company.

No man to give up, Lear at the age of 73 launched one more ambitious project. In 1976, he began work on the Lear Fan 2100, a revolutionary six-passenger businessman's plane that would use two turbine engines to drive a 90-inch pusher propeller mounted at the rear of the craft. The ultralight 2100 was designed both for speed and economy—and was expected to be cheaper to operate than anything of its size on the market.

Bill Lear died of leukemia in 1978, just as the plane was coming off the drawing boards at his new firm, LearAvia. His widow, Moya Olsen Lear, honored his deathbed wish and used the proceeds from his $100 million estate to finish the project. The 2100 flew for the first time on New Year's Day, 1981—with 180 orders already on the books.

Bill Lear, in the cockpit of one of his own Learjets, displays the resolve that enabled him to become the first man in aviation history to design, build and win certification for a jet—all with his own money. "I'd annihilate my grandmother to save a pound," he once said of his determination to produce a lightweight plane.

The Model 25 Learjet, powered by two General Electric turbojet engines, cruises at 528 mph at an altitude of 51,000 feet. Certified in 1967, Model 25 was the first stretched version of the basic Learjet airframe, four feet longer than the original, with an eight-passenger capacity.

A Lear Fan 2100 is assembled at LearAvia headquarters in Reno, Nevada. Weighing only 4,000 pounds, the 2100 can cruise at a speed of 350 mph for 2,000 miles on just under 250 gallons of fuel.

the pilots, who had miscalculated when to apply power and arrest descent. In the wake of the crashes, airlines established firm regulations about how great a sink rate was permissible during final approach and landing, and the crashes ceased.

With its good name restored, the 727 went on to win fame as the most successful commercial transport in history. By the time a new generation of airliners was ready to replace it in the early 1980s, nearly 2,000 Boeing 727s had been sold or ordered. That Boeing could sell so many is all the more remarkable because the 727 did not have the market to itself for long. Its $4.2 million price was too steep for many small companies that flew short hops, and the plane was uneconomical for larger airlines to operate on similar routes. What was needed was a still smaller airplane, and into this gap stepped the dogged British and mighty Douglas.

Despite the Trident's promise, the plane turned out to be a disappointment. Production delays had allowed the 727 to beat it into service. Moreover, the Trident carried too few passengers to compete with the 727. With sales of the Trident languishing, the newly formed British Aircraft Corporation—the Air Ministry had finally succeeded in consolidating the aircraft industry—set its sights on a short-range jet. It would be a small craft that, with two engines mounted at the tail instead of three, would be profitable in short-haul service.

On May 9, 1961, BAC—even though it had only one order for 10 of the new planes—bravely announced that the One-Eleven, as the airliner was designated, would go into production. Originally, the specifications had called for about 80 seats and a range of up to 1,600 miles. Had such a plane been built, it would have had capabilities virtually identical to the Trident's, but having one fewer engine, it would have been cheaper to operate. However, the airliner was scaled down to curtail production costs and wound up with only 65 seats and a much shorter range—less than 900 miles.

This was a crucial error; the One-Eleven would be seen as too small. But for the moment at least there was no competitor in sight save the Caravelle. Indeed, a wave of early U.S. orders for the One-Eleven—30 planes for American Airlines alone—convinced BAC that it had a money-making successor to the turboprop Viscount, the only British transport to have invaded the American market successfully.

Unknown to the British, Douglas was about to enter the lists. Four years earlier, when the company had canceled its four-engined DC-9 project, it already had a smaller, twin-engined jetliner on the drawing boards. Called Model 2011, the plane was the product of an engineering team headed by John Brizendine, who years later would become Douglas' president. But after United ordered 20 Caravelles from Sud Aviation, Douglas reconsidered its effort and decided that the way to address the market was as the French company's U.S. sales agent. The partnership proved to be a failure—Douglas managed to lease

Two technicians prepare a model of the DC-9 twin-jet for wind tunnel testing. As a result of such tests, Douglas increased the tail's size by one fifth to improve the plane's stability and maneuverability.

only a small number of Caravelles to TWA—and the contract was canceled after two years.

By then, Donald Douglas found himself under pressure from within his own company to get into the short-range competition. Much of it was coming from Jackson R. McGowen, a crack engineer and salesman credited with snaring many DC-8 orders. He pointed out that the company already had on hand plans for the Model 2011 and that the plane had caught the fancy of Delta Airlines' president Woolman. On April 8, without a single contract in-house, Douglas announced that it would build Model 2011 as the DC-9. The step was a bold one, and it kept Douglas in the transport business. In May Woolman signed an order for 15 DC-9s.

The plane would turn out to be larger than the BAC One-Eleven, but smaller than the 727, with its powerful Pratt & Whitney JT8D engines mounted near the tail on either side of the fuselage. Easy maintenance and a two-man flight-deck crew—one man less than flew the 727—promised the lowest operating costs of any airliner yet.

Douglas had beaten Boeing to the punch. Not until early 1965, only three days before the DC-9's first flight, did Boeing announce that it would manufacture its own short-range jetliner, the 737. The plane's design was influenced greatly by the requirements of Lufthansa, the first airline to place an order for it. The Germans insisted on a passenger capacity of at least 100—10 more than the DC-9 could accommodate. The only way that Boeing could fulfill this requirement was to give the 737 the same width as the 727 and 707. Shorter by 10 feet than the DC-9, the stubby 737 resembled a beer barrel with wings.

Boeing's entry into the short-range contest, even though it came late, clearly outstripped the BAC One-Eleven in power and approached the DC-9 in economy. Airlines liked the width of the 737 fuselage, which allowed six-abreast seating instead of the DC-9's five. But unfortunately for Boeing, the 737 ran afoul of the Air Line Pilots Association. ALPA had not objected to a two-pilot complement for the BAC One-Eleven; there simply was not room in the cockpit for a third crew member. Nor had the union insisted that the DC-9 carry a three-man crew; before ALPA could specify otherwise, Delta's pilots had agreed to operate the DC-9 with two pilots only. But by the time the 737 entered airline service in 1968, ALPA demanded that the plane be flown by three pilots, even though the third would have little to do.

The policy hurt 737 sales for several years; the expense of a redundant crew member raised the 737's operating costs and made the plane unacceptable to many airlines, particularly to rapidly expanding but small companies like North Central Airlines (it became Republic Airlines in 1979), which flew between Minneapolis and Denver and between Duluth and Chicago. However, the worldwide fuel crisis in 1974, combined with a recession and increased competition among the airlines, forced ALPA to abandon its three-man policy, and 737 sales immediately picked up.

Small jetliners like the DC-9 and 737 brought the jet revolution to towns and cities that hitherto had been served by piston-powered planes, and they spawned a steady growth in air travel that helped create giant airlines out of onetime midgets. Allegheny Airlines, for example, began a transformation with the purchase of its first small jets in 1965. In 14 years, it would outgrow its name and become USAir, carrying more passengers than Pan Am, operating more daily flights than TWA and serving more cities than American.

With the proliferation of 737s, DC-9s and, to a lesser extent, BAC One-Elevens, the jets had at last fulfilled the potential envisioned for them by Eddie Rickenbacker in 1955. Airliners, taking off and landing as often as once a minute from airports like O'Hare in Chicago, Heathrow in London and Orly in Paris, crisscrossed the countries of the world like airborne trains, transporting millions of passengers billions of miles each year. Yet almost before the airlines and their customers had become fully accustomed to the new order, even more remarkable jet aircraft were discernible just ahead. 〜〜

On November 29, 1973, proud workers at the Boeing plant in Renton, Washington, celebrate the roll-out of the 1,000th 727 jetliner. The forward part of the fuselage was emblazoned with a sampling of the logos seen here, representing the airlines and other companies throughout the world that were then operating 727s.

Workhorses for the short haul

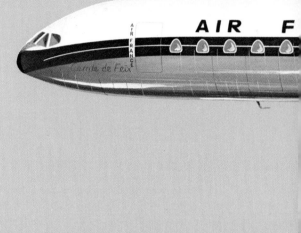

"I'm leavin' on a jet plane," ran the words of a popular 1960s song, a refrain that captured the public's enthusiastic endorsement of this rapid new means of travel. Yet jet speed and comfort were not immediately available to everyone. The earliest commercial jets operated profitably only over long-distance routes, and they could not land on or take off from the limited runways of smaller airports.

By mid-decade, however, plane makers had come up with a second generation of jetliners specifically designed for shorter hops. Within a few years, the short-haulers had largely replaced propeller-driven passenger aircraft in American and European skies.

The workhorse demands of the short-haul market forced designers to modify basic concepts of airplane design. The French Caravelle, for example, surprised the aviation world with its two engines mounted at the rear of the fuselage, an arrangement that had distinct advantages for a modern passenger jet. Apart from making for a quieter cabin, it allowed flaps to be fitted across the entire wingspan, dramatically improving short runway performance. Douglas designers adopted an almost identical twin-engined arrangement a few years later for the DC-9.

Both the British Hawker Siddeley Trident and the Boeing 727 had three tail-mounted engines. The third engine gave the planes extra flexibility in terms of range and safety—an important consideration for carriers that flew over bodies of water. For reasons of economy, Boeing returned to a twin-engined design for its stubby 737, mounting the turbojets conventionally under each wing. And the company's more recent 757, a larger, advanced-technology aircraft expected to operate well into the 21st Century, also has two engines, slung from pylons.

The airliners shown here and on the following pages are in relative scale. The year given next to the model number is the first date of commercial service.

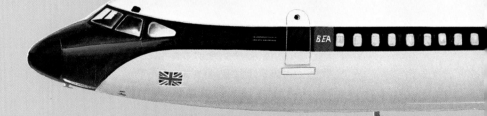

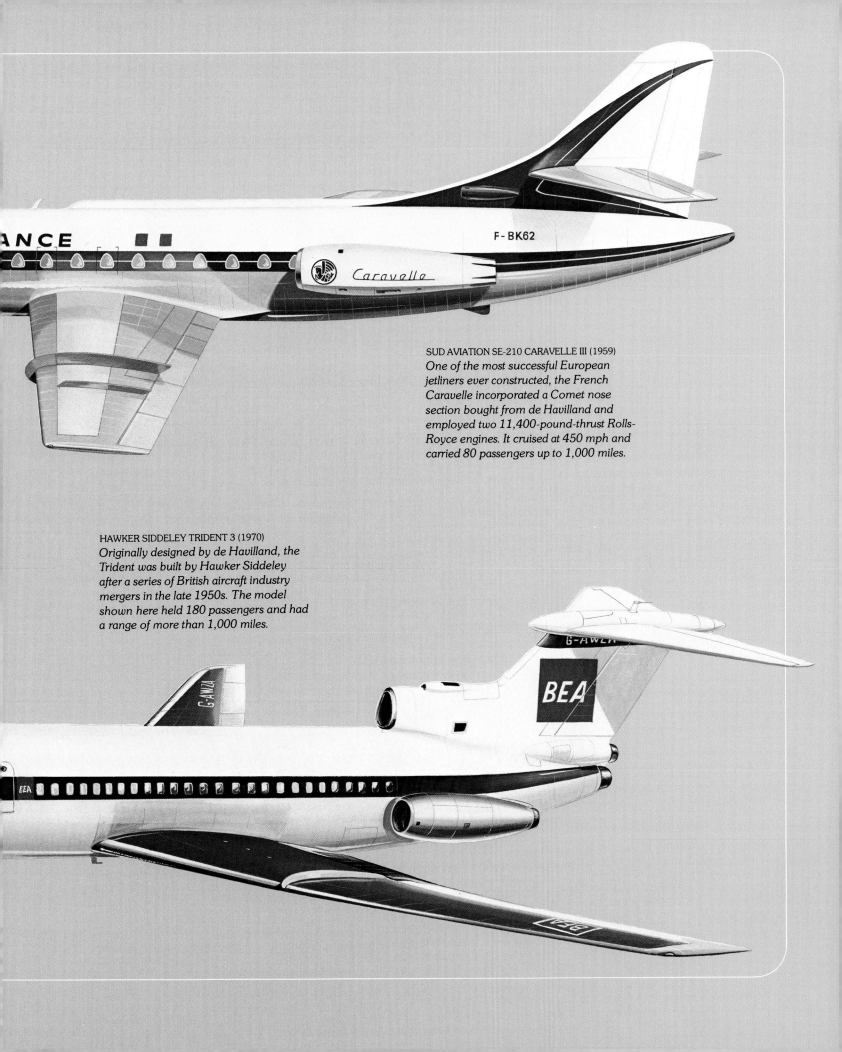

SUD AVIATION SE-210 CARAVELLE III (1959)
One of the most successful European jetliners ever constructed, the French Caravelle incorporated a Comet nose section bought from de Havilland and employed two 11,400-pound-thrust Rolls-Royce engines. It cruised at 450 mph and carried 80 passengers up to 1,000 miles.

HAWKER SIDDELEY TRIDENT 3 (1970)
Originally designed by de Havilland, the Trident was built by Hawker Siddeley after a series of British aircraft industry mergers in the late 1950s. The model shown here held 180 passengers and had a range of more than 1,000 miles.

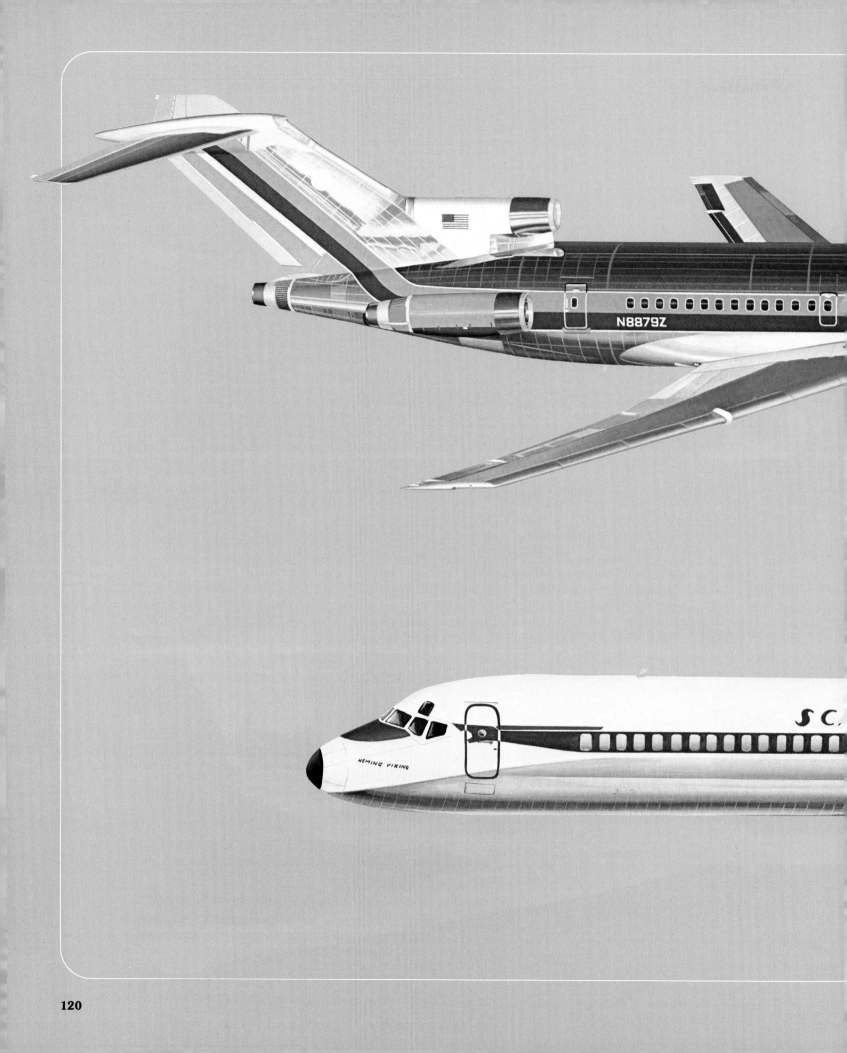

N8879Z

HEMING VIKING

SCA

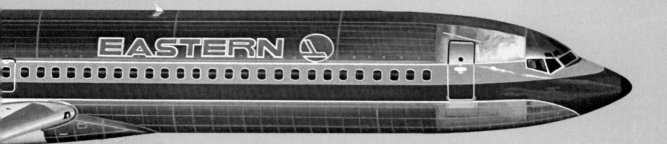

BOEING 727-200 (1964)
Powered by three 14,500-pound-thrust turbofan engines, the 727 was the first American trijet and became the world's best-selling airliner. It seats up to 131 passengers and has a range of 2,500 miles.

MCDONNELL-DOUGLAS DC-9 SRS.40 (1966)
Designed along lines similar to the Caravelle's, the DC-9 quickly outstripped the French jet in sales, even though it appeared several years later. Powered by two 15,500-pound-thrust engines, it carried 125 passengers up to 1,670 miles.

BOEING 737-100 (1968)
The smallest Boeing passenger jet, the 737 is an economical short-hauler that has the same fuselage width as the 707 and 727. This early version could carry up to 100 passengers on routes of 700 miles.

BOEING 757-200 (1983)
Powered by two 37,000-pound-thrust turbofan engines, the 757 incorporates weight-saving materials in its structure and features an electronic instrument system that displays flight data on color video-tube screens. It carries up to 218 passengers and has a 2,000-mile range.

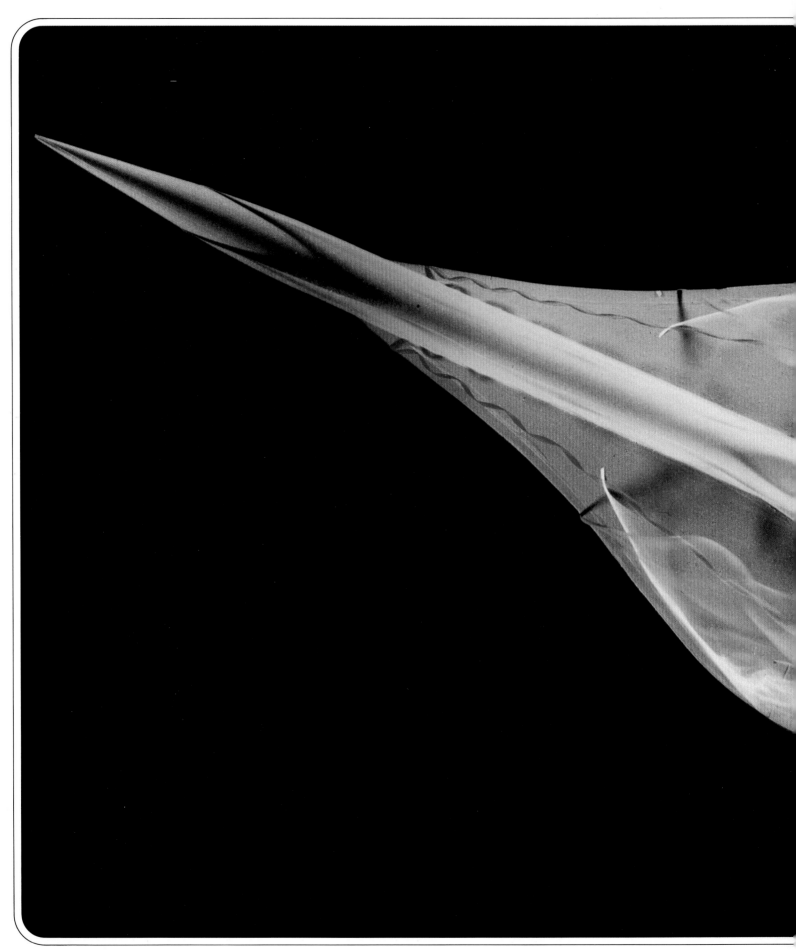

Colored dyes simulate airflow patterns on a scale model of the supersonic Concorde that has been submerged for tests in streaming water.

The fastest—and the biggest

In September 1962, a Citroen sedan pulled up at an old factory on the outskirts of Paris. The building had once been owned by Louis Blériot, the French aviation pioneer who in 1909 was the first to fly the English Channel; now it belonged to Sud Aviation, builders of the Caravelle. Out of the car stepped Lucien Servanty, Sud Aviation's chief designer, and his counterpart at the British Aircraft Corporation, Dr. William Strang.

The two men walked into the building, found an empty office and locked the door. Hours later they emerged with a set of preliminary designs for the first airliner to fly faster than the speed of sound. It was aptly named the Concorde, for the project would demand the ultimate in aeronautical cooperation between France and Great Britain.

Across the Atlantic, meanwhile, the huge and enormously successful American aircraft industry was beginning to move in an entirely different direction—toward much larger airliners, not faster ones. The United States Air Force had started the trend in 1962 by giving a contract to Lockheed for a giant cargo plane called the C-141 Starlifter. A fuselage 145 feet long and four 21,000-pound-thrust turbofans enabled the transport to carry nearly 71,000 pounds of troops and equipment more than 4,000 miles nonstop. A plane of similar capacity might appeal to airlines; projections indicated that traffic would soon exceed 100 million passengers a year, and fleets of mammoth airliners would be needed to handle such volume. But it would be Boeing, not Lockheed, that would first rise to the challenge with a fantastic jumbo jet known simply by the numerals 747.

Thus the stage was set for a two-pronged assault on the future. One path would lead to the swiftest commercial aircraft ever placed in regular service, the other to the largest. At the outset, both directions seemed to promise great profits. Speed was the essence of air travel. Were not jetliners already well on the way to supplanting slower piston-engined aircraft? And bigger planes, as long as there were passengers to fill them, had so far proved vastly more profitable than the smaller ones that preceded them. No seer could predict that in the end only one of the endeavors—the jumbo jet—would succeed, stimulating competition among aircraft manufacturers to create similar airliners. For a variety of reasons, the supersonic project would wither; the Concorde would remain a superb technological triumph, but, sadly, a money-losing aircraft that nobody really wanted, not even its British and French developers.

It seemed to make eminent sense in 1962 for the British and French, hotly competitive in most matters, to cooperate on the Concorde. Both nations understood the necessity of countering what French President Charles de Gaulle described as the "American colonization of the skies." Each had decided independently of the other to build a supersonic transport as a way of breaking the United States monopoly but had been stymied by the expense. Better for the two nations to share the development costs—and the profits, when they came—than not to proceed at all.

There were pressing political reasons as well as economic ones for the British to collaborate. Having at first refrained from joining the Common Market, to go it alone, Britain was now having second thoughts. It saw its participation in the creation of the supersonic transport as an opportunity to prove to France, which could veto its admission to the Market, that it could be a reliable and valuable partner.

Servanty's and Strang's cooperation at the old Blériot factory had been the first step in the development of a supersonic jetliner. Now some formal accord was needed. This was soon worked out, and on November 29, 1962, the Anglo-French Supersonic Aircraft Agreement was signed. The development of the plane—and the entire bill for it—was to be shared equally by the French and British governments; Sud Aviation and the British Aircraft Corporation would not risk a sou or a shilling. And as an indication of both nations' sincerity, there was no cancellation clause.

The announcement of the Anglo-French accord caused little stir in the United States. American plane builders had abandoned the idea of a supersonic transport. They knew that such an airliner could not be developed in the United States, any more than it could in Europe, without government backing. The expense was simply too high. The Air Force had in service a supersonic medium bomber, the Convair B-58, and had contracted with North American to build three prototypes of a larger one, the XB-70. Had the XB-70 been successful, it might have paved the way for a supersonic airliner, but in 1961, the Department of Defense canceled the project. One prototype was never finished, one was destroyed in a mid-air collision and the third was put on display at the Air Force Museum in Dayton, Ohio.

Thus, the French and British took the lead by default and ran little risk of losing it, even though it was May of 1963 before detailed drawings for the Concorde were far enough advanced for work to begin on two prototypes, one in France and one in England. Ostensibly, two planes were needed to give both countries experience in building an SST and to expedite flight testing, which was expected to get under way sometime in 1967. But the two prototypes also betrayed the undercurrent of suspicion between the French and the British; each feared that the other would somehow contrive to take all the credit for the Concorde.

The prototypes were designed to carry 118 passengers at a cruising speed of Mach 2.2, slightly more than twice the speed of sound, or 1,450 miles per hour at a cruising altitude of 50,000 feet—but no faster. A speed limit was necessary if the aircraft was not to heat up excessively in flight. Even in the−94° temperature and thin atmosphere where the Concorde would cruise, a plane exceeding Mach 2.2 would become so hot from friction that it would have to be constructed of a metal more heat resistant than aluminum, such as titanium or stainless steel. But to employ these materials would add immeasurably to its cost.

To be certain that the Concorde could endure the temperature extremes of supersonic flight, British engineers built a closely fitting casing around the fuselage and one wing of a test airframe. Through the narrow space between plane and casing, they blew hot and cold air. The test would be repeated thousands of times to prove that the aluminum would not become brittle with fatigue from thermal contraction and expansion in flight.

This was only one of many tests carried out on the airframe. The wings were the subject of particular investigation. The designers had come up with a delta shape suitable for a plane flying faster than the speed of sound. The wing was put through 5,000 hours of wind tunnel tests, and though the French balked at the delay these tests caused, the time was well invested. Even the slightest flaw in the design could have produced air resistance that might have shortened the plane's range by hundreds of miles.

As a result of the delta shape, the wings would not only be efficient for supersonic flight but would provide enough lift to allow the Concorde to land at 177 miles per hour, significantly faster than a 707. Even at that speed, however, the wings would lower the plane gently to earth only if the pilot pointed the Concorde steeply into the air—which, unfortunately, meant that he would be deprived of a view of the runway ahead of him. Here the engineers came up with an ingenious solution; they gave the plane a nose that, at the touch of a control, could be tilted downward, thus providing maximum visibility during landing.

The plane was powered by four Olympus engines built jointly in Britain and France; together they would provide more than 150,000 pounds of thrust, twice as much as the engines on a 707, whose gross weight was close to that of the Concorde.

In every respect the Concorde promised to be a technical tour de force without precedent in commercial aviation. Yet even as the prototypes took shape, first on paper and then in the hangars of Sud Aviation and BAC, the French and British were beginning to feel apprehensive about the Concorde's future. Some airlines had complained that the plane was too small. The designers responded by changing the blueprints; they stretched the fuselage by eight and one half feet and raised the number of seats to 136. But coming as late as it did, this modification could not be incorporated into the prototypes and had to await actual production of the aircraft.

Size was a problem that could at least be addressed. More worrying was the noise the Concorde's four mammoth turbojet engines would make. Quieter turbofans had been judged unsuitable for supersonic flight, since their large air intakes caused excessive drag. Without the muffling effect of fans, the Olympus engines would thunder louder on takeoff and landing than those of any other airliner. Some cities might ban the Concorde because of the noise.

But the roar of the engines was nothing compared with the effect the shock wave, or sonic boom, might have on public acceptance of the SST. Radiating outward from any plane flying faster than sound, the shock wave could shatter windows, crack walls and shake plaster from ceilings. In 1964, the Federal Aviation Administration had sponsored an experiment called Operation *Bongo Mark 2* in which Air Force B-58 supersonic bombers subjected the 324,000 inhabitants of Oklahoma City to 1,254 sonic booms over a five-month period. Before the assault ended, 15,000 complaints had been filed. A large proportion were fraudulent, but many were not; more than $200,000 had to be paid in damages. It would hardly be surprising if many countries prohibited supersonic flights over their land.

On top of these headaches came the realization that the Concorde might not be much of a seller. Early estimates had put sales at between 160 and 400 aircraft by 1980. But by March 1967, only 74 options for the aircraft had been taken by 16 airlines, including Pan Am, Air France, BOAC, Japan Air Lines and Australia's Qantas. Many of these options had been secured only because the Concorde had been redesigned to carry the more profitable payload of 136 passengers. But this change had added to the already skyrocketing projected investment costs. Further changes to satisfy the airlines' demands for more cargo space would escalate costs still higher, to more than $1.75 billion—$1.3 billion greater than the original 1962 estimate.

It soon became obvious to the British and French governments that none of the public monies expended on development were likely to be recovered. But the project went forward; national pride was involved, particularly among the French, who turned increasingly rigid the gloomier the commercial assessments became. No one wanted to admit it, but the Concorde was beginning to look distinctly like a white elephant. Even with its carrying capacity increased, it would still be transporting far fewer passengers than the intercontinental version of the Boeing 707. Worse, it would consume 20 per cent more fuel for an Atlantic crossing. Airlines would have to charge a premium for tickets, making the round-trip fare $328 higher than a first-class seat on a regular jetliner—and $1,394 higher than the tourist fares that made up the bulk of the traffic. "The Concorde," said a member of Parliament in 1966, "is not for the ordinary man in the street. It will be for the international jet set, people playing the power game on other people's money—politicians, businessmen and diplomats."

When, in 1963 and again in 1964, Britain quietly approached

One of the first color pictures of the Tu-144 prototype seen in the West delineates the spectacular S curve of the jet's wing. The Soviet designers gave the wing this shape to eliminate nose shock waves as the jet crossed the sound barrier. The wing was later modified to have straight leading edges for improved supersonic performance.

France to discuss canceling the project or altering it to save money, the French refused. The Concorde would proceed as planned, warned the French, or else. If Britain withdrew, membership in the Common Market would be even more elusive. Since there was no cancellation clause in the Concorde agreement, France could sue in the World Court and in all probability it would win, causing Britain great embarrassment. Moreover, Britain would lose all the money it had invested in the endeavor and any residual rights in the airplane if the French went ahead on their own. Short of risking all this, Britain had no choice but to go on.

Work was completed on the French prototype in August 1968 but taxi tests exposed problems with the brakes and landing gear. Not only did correcting these deficiencies cost the French and British more money, but they cost time, depriving Britain and France in the end of the prestige of being first to fly a supersonic airliner.

That distinction went to the Russians, who on December 31, 1968, rushed their Tupolev 144 into the air for its maiden flight. The Tu-144 resembled the Concorde so closely that the British dubbed it the "Concordski" and suspected the Russians of industrial espionage. Be that as it may, Soviet commercial aircraft had generally proved inefficient and uneconomical and had never posed a threat to Western manufacturers. The Tu-144 would be no exception and would soon fade from the scene (page 128 and right).

The French prototype, emblazoned with the words British Aircraft Corporation-Sud Aviation France Concorde, lifted off the runway on March 2, 1969. The flight lasted 42 minutes, and no attempt was made to exceed the speed of sound. The British prototype flew on April 9, also at subsonic speed. Both groups were being cautious. A true demonstration of the Concorde's potential would have to wait until further tests and appraisals of the plane in flight had been made.

In the meantime, on the other side of the ocean, work was getting started on the 747—in a roundabout way. In 1962, Boeing saw an opportunity for itself in the shortcomings of Lockheed's C-141 Starlifter. Maynard Pennell, the man who had so emphatically assured Bill Allen at Farnborough more than a decade earlier that the company could make a better airliner than the Comet, had his staff analyze the cargo-carrying capacity of the Starlifter. They discovered that despite the plane's mammoth size, the C-141 was short on volume; the jet would be full long before it had been loaded to its maximum takeoff weight. Pennell and his engineers proposed that Boeing undertake the design of a transport even larger than the C-141 and quickly roughed out the preliminary design of a cargo plane longer and wider than the C-141 and having 10 times the capacity.

Boeing was confident it could build such a giant. Among other things, it could apply the experience gained in developing the 727 to designing flaps that would allow the new transport to operate from existing run-

A tragic end to an air show

At first glance, the Soviet Union's supersonic transport, the Tupolev 144, appeared to be a twin of the Anglo-French Concorde. It featured a similar fuselage and sweptback wing and the same "droop-snoot" hinged nose to improve the forward view from the cockpit. So close was the resemblance that Western aeronautical engineers called the design "Concordski." The craft was slightly larger than the Concorde, with room for 121 passengers—and a bit faster, with a claimed speed of 1,500 mph.

Eager to publicize their supersonic liner, the Soviets exhibited it at the Paris Air Show in 1971 and again in 1973. At the second show it took off on a short flight and, with all eyes upon it, ran into trouble and crashed (sequence at right). The Soviets never released an official explanation of the cause of the accident.

Over the next four years subsequent models underwent extensive tests, while rumors reached the West of numerous problems, including unacceptably high fuel consumption. In November 1977, the Tu-144 went into weekly passenger service between Moscow and Alma Ata in Soviet Central Asia. But in just 10 months, the trouble-plagued craft was grounded more or less for good—again without explanation.

Dwarfing a Soviet technician, a huge model of the Tu-144 supersonic transport rests in the mouth of the vast wind tunnel at Moscow's Central Aerodynamics Institute.

A sequence of photographs shows the Soviet Tu-144's disastrous flight at the 1973 Paris Air Show. After making a low pass over the airfield, the pilot pulled the nose up sharply. The aircraft climbed to 4,500 feet, then suddenly dived earthward, its tail separating as it fell. The plane turned over, then blew up in a ball of flame, sections of it crashing on the main street of a nearby village. Seven villagers, mostly children, were killed, along with the jet's crew of six.

ways. And with an eye to an Air Force contract, Boeing made certain that the plane would have enough wheels in the main landing gear to spread the weight of the jet so that it could fly into and out of airfields with grass landing strips.

The Air Force was quick to recognize the aircraft's potential as a carrier of men and equipment to distant trouble spots and lost no time in asking Boeing to prepare a bid. But to make the situation competitive, it also called upon Douglas and Lockheed to prepare bids for a large aircraft of their own design.

Even as the three companies were laboring to meet the Air Force specifications for the plane, American interest in a supersonic transport, or SST, was being rekindled. Part of the impetus was the progress the French and British were making on the Concorde, but an even greater incentive came from what was still but a rumor in 1963: that the Soviet Union had also decided to produce a supersonic airliner. "One of the worst beatings we'll ever get," said American Airlines president C. R. Smith, "is if we have to look up to a Soviet SST, the way we had to look up to the first Sputnik."

Foremost among the SST's proponents was Najeeb Halaby, appointed by President John Kennedy to succeed Elwood Quesada at the Federal Aviation Administration. He felt that the project was so vital to American prestige that public money should finance it. Kennedy agreed. Thus on June 5, 1963, only one day after Pan Am revealed that it had taken options on eight Concordes, the President announced that the United States would develop an SST prototype. As eventually approved by Congress, the project called for the government to assume 75 per cent of the estimated $1.5 billion development costs, with the federal funds to be repaid through royalties on every SST sold. Boeing, Lockheed and North American, the builder of the XB-70, were invited to submit bids.

Now two major competitions—one for the SST and another for the giant transport, which the Air Force called the C-5A—were under way. In June 1965, having submitted the lowest bid, Lockheed was named to build the C-5A. Boeing could not conceal its disappointment over not getting the contract. From an engineering standpoint, it felt that its design was the best of the three. Rather than give up, Boeing began thinking about converting the military transport into a commercial airliner. It had some reason to feel encouraged. No less a figure in the aviation world than Pan Am's president, Juan Trippe, had indicated that he was interested in just such a plane. In fact, Pan Am officials had been working—unsuccessfully, as it turned out—with all three competitors in the C-5A contest to come up with a plane that could be adapted to commercial use.

When the announcement came that Lockheed had won the C-5A competition, Trippe immediately telephoned Lockheed to ask about the feasibility of buying a civilian model of the transport. But knowing that the C-5A would have to be completely redesigned and lacking the

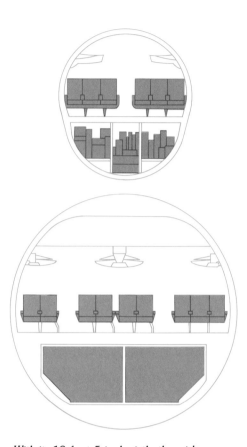

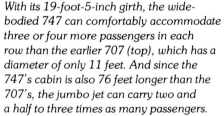

With its 19-foot-5-inch girth, the wide-bodied 747 can comfortably accommodate three or four more passengers in each row than the earlier 707 (top), which has a diameter of only 11 feet. And since the 747's cabin is also 76 feet longer than the 707's, the jumbo jet can carry two and a half to three times as many passengers.

resources to do so, the company had decided to concentrate on the SST. Nor did Douglas care to evolve a new design from its C-5A entry. This left the field open to Boeing.

At the risk of overextending itself with two blockbuster projects, the SST and a large subsonic airliner, Boeing nevertheless decided to proceed. Under the supervision of its chief of technology, Joel Sutter, the company's C-5A entry was totally reworked and designated Model 747. It would be the first of a whole category of jetliners known as widebodies. The plane, as finally conceived, was to measure 19 feet 5 inches across. Its width and its 231-foot length would provide room for 450 seats—nearly two and a half times as many as the 707. Moreover, the 747 would be 30 per cent cheaper to operate than the 707 and DC-8, and at 625 miles per hour, faster as well.

Trippe was suitably impressed. On April 13, 1966, he signed a letter of intent to buy 25 of the jumbo jets. The price of this fleet was $525 million, more than any company had ever paid for the purchase of a single type of airliner.

Then on December 31, Boeing received more good news. Its proposal for a supersonic transport had won government approval and the project was to begin at once.

Boeing's efforts to design an SST got off to a good start but soon bogged down. The company came up with an innovative design for wings that could be swung from almost perpendicular to the fuselage for takeoff and landing to a sharply sweptback position for supersonic flight. Not only would such an arrangement make the airliner more efficient at subsonic speeds; it would make it quieter—less power being required for takeoff. But there was a snag.

The wings would swing on two huge pivots, 36 inches in diameter. The pivots, together with the machinery required to move the wings, would weigh 40,000 pounds, even if made of lightweight titanium. Their weight might have been offset by the exceptional efficiency of the wings, but wind tunnel tests and computer analyses revealed deficiencies in the airworthiness of the design that could be corrected only by adding stubby wings, called canards, to the nose section, thus increasing the plane's weight still more.

Engineers pored over the SST blueprints and whittled away about 23,000 pounds. Hard though they tried, they were unable to keep the SST from being more than 50,000 pounds overweight. "Instead of entering into a situation where the problems began to offset one another," said Edward Wells, chairman of Boeing's SST Technical Advisory Council, of the plane at this point, "the problems were actually compounding." Shortly thereafter, it became evident that the swing-wing would never work and would have to be replaced by a simpler, fixed delta wing. Fortunately, when Boeing sought a contract extension to change the wing design, the FAA agreed.

Boeing's other project—the 747—was also running into problems, some having to do with its size. The plane would make Lilliputians of all

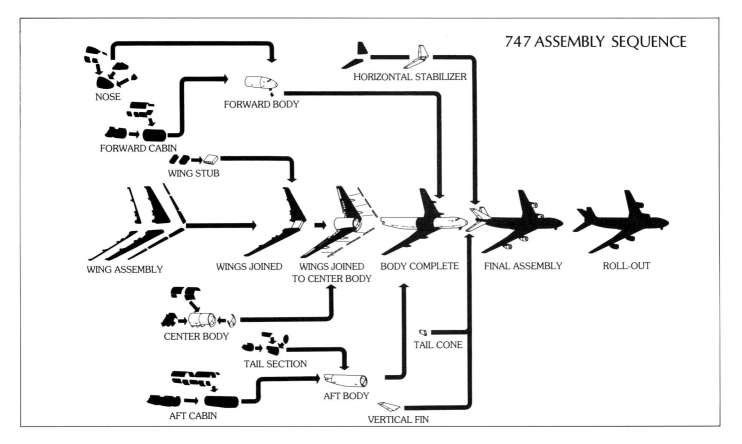

747 ASSEMBLY SEQUENCE

NOSE

FORWARD BODY

HORIZONTAL STABILIZER

FORWARD CABIN

WING STUB

WING ASSEMBLY

WINGS JOINED

WINGS JOINED TO CENTER BODY

BODY COMPLETE

FINAL ASSEMBLY

ROLL-OUT

CENTER BODY

TAIL SECTION

TAIL CONE

AFT BODY

AFT CABIN

VERTICAL FIN

existing jetliners. The fuselage was to be almost as long as a football field. The tail would reach as high as a six-story building. A seven-foot basketball player could stand in the mouth of one of the four Pratt & Whitney JT9D 41,000-pound-thrust turbofans with a foot of headroom to spare. The wings spanned 195 feet 8 inches. So enormous was the 747 that it would require an acre of parking space.

Taking its overwhelming size into account, some people jokingly referred to the 747 as the "Aluminum Overcoat" and the "Big Ugly." Others—particularly Boeing's executives—were concerned about the effect that one crash would have on public consciousness. The mind-boggling statistics—450 passengers and 18 crew members dead—caused sober reflection, and Boeing went to extraordinary lengths to make the 747 safe. It appointed a safety committee, consisting of five members, to consider every aspect of the aircraft. The committee insisted on four main hydraulic systems, three of them to serve as backups. It pushed for an undercarriage so strong that the plane could land safely if two of the four main landing gears malfunctioned. Wings were built to support a load 50 per cent greater than the jet would normally be expected to carry.

Concern for passenger safety extended to the inside of the plane as well. The 747 made extensive use of flame-resistant, nontoxic materials for the cabin wall lining. The railing of the spiral staircase leading to the upper-level lounge was moved farther from the wall to avoid the possibility of a passenger getting an arm caught between railing and wall

As this construction-sequence diagram from Boeing shows, the 747 assembly line begins with the putting together of the wings. When this is done, other sections of the plane are added to them in a process that takes only about 45 days to complete.

Front and rear sections of a 747 are delivered to the final assembly area from other parts of the plant by an overhead crane. They will be lowered onto adjustable cradles (one can be seen under the nose) for precise alignment with the core of the airplane, then riveted in place.

during sudden turbulence. The five safety specialists even examined the coffee makers to ensure that drain outlets were located far enough away from wiring to avoid short circuits.

As the designers worked on the plane, they realized that it was beginning to suffer from the same affliction as the SST—it was gaining weight rapidly. They did everything possible—Boeing even sponsored a contest among employees to pare it down. A revamped wing shaved off 1,000 pounds. Heavy paper impregnated with Nomex (a new, flameproof du Pont plastic) was used for certain external parts that would be exposed to little stress, lightening the load still more. And in another weight-reducing measure the immense main landing gear beams, nine feet in length, were made of titanium.

When it came to building the 747, Boeing was confronted by another headache. With orders from Pan Am, United, Air France and others on the books, it had no plant big enough to assemble its giant and had to construct a new one near Everett, Washington. The building would sprawl over 780 acres of land adjacent to a county airport with a runway long enough to handle the jet. And in order for the 747 to roll out on schedule, Boeing had to begin building components of the plane long before the complex was complete.

On February 9, 1969, the first 747 was ready for its inaugural flight. Excitement ran high as hundreds of spectators lined the runway. Boeing's chief test pilot, Jack Waddell, took it all in stride. "I don't know how you can glamorize it," he said later, "I had a good night's sleep near Everett at a motel the night before, got up and had a waffle and some sausages, my favorite, and went out to the airplane." For Waddell, the flight was just another day's work, although it ended prematurely when the flaps caused unexpected vibrations. There was no danger, but to avoid damaging the new aircraft, Waddell brought the 747 back in. "The plane handles beautifully," he said after landing. "I'd call it a two-finger airplane; you can fly it with the forefinger and thumb on the wheel."

The problem with the flaps—they had been misaligned during installation—was quickly rectified, and the 747 underwent further

Undergoing stress tests, the wing of the 747 prototype becomes a blur as the main spar, bent upward 26 feet by powerful hydraulic jacks, gives way. Heavy rope netting hangs over the scaffolding to catch any parts that may spring loose.

flight tests. While these were going on, pilots from airlines that had ordered 747s attended the Boeing Airline Training School in Seattle. There they spent hours learning to fly the plane in a computer-controlled simulator.

To give the pilots the experience of what it would feel like to taxi around an airport in the giant aircraft, a unique device called "Waddell's Wagon" was brought into play (Waddell had actually helped design it). It featured a truck with three-story stilts mounted on it. Perched atop the stilts was the shell of a 747 flight deck, and there the pilot sat, directing the driver of the truck by radio. One pilot likened the experience to "sitting on the roof of my house and trying to drive the thing into the street."

After years of expectation and build-up, the first scheduled 747 flight proved something of an embarrassment. Following a short inauguration ceremony in a terminal at New York's Kennedy Airport, the 336 Europe-bound passengers boarded the Pan Am plane, christened the *Clipper Young America*. There was a delay of several minutes as the flight crew struggled to close a balky door. Then 25 more minutes elapsed before the ground crew had loaded all 15 tons of cargo into the hold. When *Young America* finally taxied to the end of the runway for takeoff, the pilot, 26-year veteran Bob Weeks, noticed that an engine was overheating. He had no choice but to return to the terminal. Pan Am had another 747 standing by, but by the time it was prepared for flight, loaded with *Young America's* cargo and passengers, seven hours had gone by. The 747, originally scheduled to depart at 7 p.m., finally took off at two in the morning.

Such a beginning might have been read as an omen. The airlines, it turned out, were initially disappointed with the 747. Because of the plane's weight, pilots were forced to run the engines at a higher power setting, causing overheating. This led to more repairs—and to higher maintenance costs than had been expected. Two years would go by before Pratt & Whitney could increase the thrust of the JT9D turbofan and cure the problem.

As if all this had not been disheartening enough to the airlines, the growth in air travel that had been predicted four years earlier when they had signed up for 747s was slow to materialize because of an economic recession. The airlines suddenly faced the prospect of hundreds of seats they could not fill.

Passengers themselves were not particularly enthusiastic about the plane. Engine problems often delayed flights. Waiting lines for the airliner's 12 lavatories would sometimes stretch down the aisles. Food service was often erratic because flight attendants were unaccustomed to serving so many passengers. Charles Lindbergh, a Pan Am board member, reported that on an early transatlantic flight the harried cabin attendants took so long serving dinner that they never got around to serving breakfast. After a 747 landed, it disgorged an avalanche of luggage that overwhelmed the baggage-handling capa-

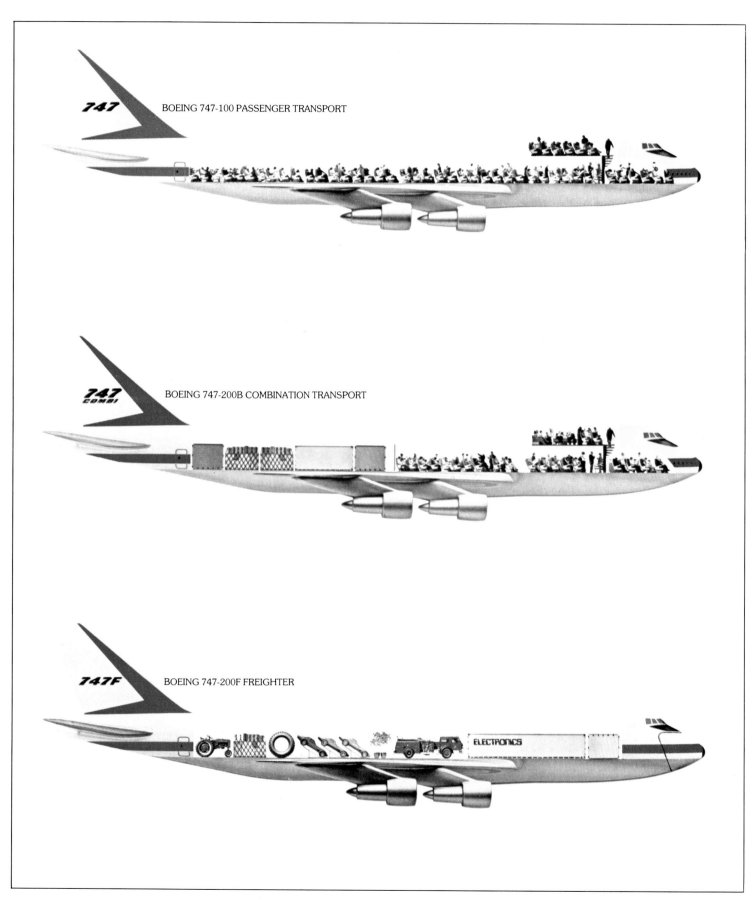

747 BOEING 747-100 PASSENGER TRANSPORT

747 COMBI BOEING 747-200B COMBINATION TRANSPORT

747F BOEING 747-200F FREIGHTER

ELECTRONICS

bilities of many airports and left passengers waiting half an hour or more for their bags.

Gradually, these problems were ironed out, and the flying public began to appreciate the 747's advantages—its roominess, the wide seats even in coach, the upstairs lounge. Pan Am turned the lounge into a restaurant for first-class passengers; they could board a 747 and then "go out to dinner." Continental Air Lines outfitted the coach section with a bar and featherweight piano, complete with pianist, to serenade passengers.

The problems that Boeing had with the 747 were nothing compared with those that the company's SST project presented. Public opposition to the idea of a supersonic plane had mounted as the project wore on. In 1967, Dr. William Shurcliff, a Harvard University scientist, organized the Citizens League Against the Sonic Boom. Soon, the group began to distribute arguments condemning supersonic flights over populated areas. Other scientists hypothesized that the exhaust from SSTs, expelled into the atmosphere at high altitude, would start a self-perpetuating chemical reaction that would ultimately deplete a radiation-absorbing layer of ozone in the stratosphere and bring on an increase in skin cancer.

Few of these claims were anything more than poorly documented conjecture, but they were enough to incite the public against the SST. As resistance grew, Congress began to express doubts about the plane. President Richard Nixon, shortly after he was elected in 1968, appointed a 12-member committee to report on the project. Believing like Presidents Kennedy and Johnson before him that the plane was essential to American prestige, Nixon hoped that the committee's report would be a favorable one. Instead, it blasted the SST not only on environmental grounds but on economic ones as well. Three billion dollars would be spent before the first SST came off the assembly line, and at best the government would not recover its investment until 300 aircraft had been sold. When the committee's report became public, it all but sealed the fate of the SST, but not before additional millions of dollars had been sunk into the project. The plane was finally killed on May 20, 1971, just about two years after the Concorde prototypes had first flown.

In Europe, the cancellation of the American SST cut two ways. British and French proponents of supersonic air travel feared that the Concorde might run afoul of the same sentiments that helped scuttle Boeing's SST. But they also knew that they now had the supersonic field all to themselves. "The Concorde program," said Henri Ziegler, president of Aérospatiale, "must be pursued with more energy and confidence than ever." For this to happen, the options taken by the airlines on the Concorde would have to be converted into sales.

So far, not a single company had given sign of ordering one. Then in July 1972, BOAC, with eight options, agreed to purchase five

Three cutaways of the 747 demonstrate the jet's versatility. At top is the conventional passenger plane, with a full 450-seat load. In the middle is the so-called Combi, which can be converted to a 6- or 12-container cargo plane in as little as 11 hours. And at bottom is an all-cargo 747, fitted with a special swing-up nose door; the all-cargo version holds as many as 29 outsized containers.

British-built Concordes; Air France, also with eight options, signed up for four to be assembled in Toulouse. Only the small size of the orders came as a surprise; BOAC and Air France, as flag airlines of governments that had invested millions in the plane, had no choice but to order the Concorde.

For the world to be convinced of the Concorde's potential, a foreign airline would have to commit to the plane, and Pan Am was viewed as the likeliest—and most important—candidate. The French and British calculated that no international airline could afford to be without Concordes once this influential carrier bought them.

The assignment of making the sale went to the British. The task would not be easy. For one thing, Juan Trippe, who had founded the airline and who had been so quick to respond to each new development in aviation, had retired, and the company was now run by Charles William Seawell, formerly president of the U.S. division of Rolls-Royce Aero Engines, Incorporated. Moreover, time was running out; Pan Am's options were due to expire on January 31, 1973. BAC's sales team, under Geoffrey Knight, head of the company's commercial aircraft division, was well aware that Pan Am had just invested heavily in Boeing 747s. Suspecting that the airline could not afford Concorde for the moment, Knight hoped to keep negotiations alive by persuading Pan Am to extend its options.

When BAC's sales team sat down with Pan Am executives in New York, they produced a market survey of businessmen who flew regularly to Europe. The results showed that these travelers would

A full-scale mock-up of Boeing's SST awaits inspection by a Congressional budget committee at the company's Developmental Center in Seattle. When the Senate voted to scrap the entire SST project, the mock-up, which cost $11 million, was sold at auction for $31,000 and taken to Florida, where it was turned into a tourist attraction.

willingly pay extra for the speed offered by the Concorde—just half the time it would take another jetliner to cover the same distance. But Pan Am could not be persuaded that this enthusiasm would offset both the high price of the airliner—$65 million against $21 million for a 747—and its much higher operating costs.

Pan Am made up its mind not to buy. "When the news finally broke," recalled one member of Knight's sales team, "I heard it on the phone from Geoffrey, who told us not to be too disappointed. I put the phone down, kicked a few things and swore a few times to let off steam. Then I went and joined the others to go out and get sloshed."

Hope of selling the Concorde to any but a few airlines seemed now to have evaporated. Within a month all but two of the companies holding options on the plane allowed them to lapse, and neither of these two— Qantas and Japan Air Lines—had the courage actually to go ahead and order the plane for itself; they extended their options, but they would never use them. BOAC and Air France would be going it alone.

In the interim, two more Concordes had been built, one in France, the other in Britain. Incorporating the changes the airlines had originally insisted on, these were preproduction versions of the plane and would be used to satisfy civil aviation authorities that the Concorde performed as promised and was safe to fly at speeds faster than sound. As part of a publicity campaign, the two were flown to cities all over the world. Britain's aircraft visited the Middle East and Australia. France's touched down in Brazil, Peru, Colombia, Venezuela and on September 20, 1973, in Texas for the dedication of the new Dallas-Fort Worth International Airport. Thousands turned out in Texas to see the plane and walk through it. Local dignitaries were taken up for supersonic junkets over the Gulf of Mexico. "Everyone agrees Concorde's a show stopper," wrote the *Dallas Times Herald.*

Nine months later, as the publicity visits continued, Aérospatiale staged a dramatic demonstration of the Concorde's marvelous speed. At 8:22 a.m., June 17, 1974, the French plane took off from Boston's Logan International Airport and screamed eastward toward Paris. The takeoff had been timed to coincide with the departure of an Air France Boeing 747 from Paris, bound for Boston. When the airliners met over the Atlantic, the 747 was 620 miles out of Paris; the Concorde was nearly 2,400 miles from Boston. After landing at the French capital, the Concorde spent an hour and eight minutes refueling, then headed back west. It arrived in Boston 11 minutes ahead of the 747.

Feats like this enchanted the public but left the airlines unmoved. They believed that the plane would lose money, even though the manufacturers asserted that Pan Am and TWA together stood to lose $200 million worth of first-class transatlantic passengers a year to the Concorde as soon as it started flying the ocean regularly. The only way to convince the airlines of the plane's worth, it seemed, would be to show the doubtful how the Concorde performed in everyday operation.

A plan was developed for British Airways (the result of a merger in 1972 between BOAC and BEA) and Air France to inaugurate regular Concorde service in early 1976 between London and Bahrain on the Persian Gulf and between Paris and Buenos Aires, Argentina. But for the airlines to turn a profit, they would have to tap the bustling traffic between Europe and the United States as well. And here they faced a hurdle.

When they applied to the FAA for permission to begin Concorde service to Boston, Washington, D.C., and New York, hearings were held in these cities to assess the effect of the airplane on people and the environment. Sonic booms had already been outlawed in the United States. Now the Concorde's opponents attacked the airliner mercilessly on the ground that its engines were too noisy. The outcry took on aspects of mass hysteria. Citizens' groups protested. "It is absolutely abhorrent to us," declared the leader of an organization named Concorde Alert. "We won't tolerate it. Scratch it and rip it out!" John Kenneth Galbraith, the economist, added his voice to the chorus of dissenters when he wrote in a letter to the London *Times,* "There isn't a chance approaching that of an icicle in hell that the Concorde will ever be allowed to touch down in American airports."

But the British defended the plane, demolishing many of the opposition's arguments as irrational, misinformed or simply venal. In the end, a compromise was worked out; British Airways and Air France could fly the Concorde into Washington and New York on a 16-month trial. No sooner had the agreement been reached than the Environmental Defense Fund sued the government in an effort to overturn the decision. The effort failed, leaving a bitter taste in the mouths of the plane's detractors. "This is a sad day for our people," lamented Carol Berman of the Emergency Coalition to Stop the SST, "to realize the Government has betrayed them like this."

On the 21st of January, 1976, fourteen seemingly interminable years after Britain and France signed the agreement to build the Concorde,

A parachute billows from the tail of a Concorde prototype to slow it after landing. Installed as insurance that the sleek, fast-moving plane could be stopped before it reached the end of the runway, the parachute proved to be unnecessary and was omitted from later models.

Sparkling in the sun, Britain's Concorde prototype, carrying 12 tons of electronic monitoring devices in the cabin, undergoes a test flight. After nearly seven years of experimental service, the plane was finally retired in 1976 to the Royal Naval Air Museum at Yeovilton, England.

the plane at last entered commercial service. An Air France flight took off from Paris bound for Buenos Aires by way of Dakar on the west coast of Africa; at the same time, a British Airways Concorde departed London for Bahrain.

The route to Bahrain took the British Airways Concorde, flying at subsonic speed to prevent sonic boom, across Europe to Venice, at the top of the Adriatic Sea, in one hour and 20 minutes. Over the water, the plane accelerated at full throttle and began to climb. Passengers felt two gentle jolts as the pilot fired the two pairs of afterburners—devices that temporarily increase thrust 25 per cent by converting a jet engine's exhaust pipe into a combustion chamber. Apart from these jolts there was no other sensation to show that the plane had exceeded the speed of sound. The only sure sign was the Machmeter at the front of the cabin as its numbers changed from .99 to 1.00, the speed of sound.

"Halfway down the Adriatic," wrote Brian Calvert, copilot on the

143

Supersonic marvel

"After years of looking at it from every possible angle I am still not sure I can pin down its exact shape," wrote former Concorde pilot Brian Calvert. "Flying overhead at a few thousand feet it is slender, feminine, dart-like. On final approach it suggests a bird coming in to land. Just after landing, with its nose still down, it might be some prehistoric monster with curious eating habits."

One thing certain about the shape of the Concorde is that every line, curve and twist of the supersonic craft's 84-foot wingspan and 204-foot-long fuselage represents a precisely engineered marriage of form and function. The jet's wing, an aerodynamic compromise between the requirements of high- and low-speed flight, is swept back in a double delta compound curve known as an ogive. Slung beneath it on each side in two boxlike structures are four turbojets providing 152,000 pounds of thrust.

A fantastic 34,000 gallons of fuel are stored in wing tanks. As fuel is consumed during flight, a system of pumps and valves shifts part of the fuel's weight to auxiliary tanks located fore and aft to compensate for changes in the plane's center of gravity.

Inside the Concorde's rapier-slim fuselage up to 100 travelers are seated four-abreast where they can see the plane's speed displayed on small screens called Machmeters that are mounted on the cabin walls. But passenger comfort leaves something to be desired. The seats are narrower than those in a jumbo jet's economy class section, and the windows are about the size of a paperback book. Most passengers regard these as relatively minor inconveniences, however: Said one, "You can watch the Machmeter or look at the pretty girls, eat and drink to an elegant capacity, and by that time you are there."

First put into service in 1976, the supersonic Anglo-French Concorde cruises at twice the speed of sound and has a range of 3,050 miles. The one shown above wearing British Airways colors is rendered in full flight; the Air France plane below has its nose lowered and gear extended for landing.

flight, "we reached Mach 2 at 50,000 feet." Minutes later, the plane "shot out into the Mediterranean and entered a left turn around the south of Crete." The speed and altitude of the Concorde amazed ground controllers. "At each change to a new control authority," said Calvert, "our reported altitude caused disbelief; our time to the next checkpoint was assumed to be an error." Cyprus flashed by just to the north; minutes later the plane was "in a long, wide arc over Syria when the sun set abruptly behind us."

Three hours and 37 minutes after takeoff, the Concorde touched down in Bahrain, a perfect inaugural flight. The Air France flight was no less impressive—5,741 miles from Paris to Buenos Aires in 7 hours 25 minutes, including about an hour refueling at Dakar. Four months later, both airlines began regular flights to Washington, D.C.; New York was put on the schedule in the autumn.

Those who flew on the Concorde loved the aircraft. Its slender cabin with double seats on each side of the aisle was an inch or so narrower than that of an old piston-engined Douglas DC-4, but few passengers

At the British Aircraft Corporation plant in Filton, England, four production model Concordes undergo final assembly. Many large components, such as the nose and forward section, were built by subcontractors and delivered to the plant with all systems completely installed.

complained about cramped quarters in an airplane that cut flight time in half. Businessmen in particular, whose companies generally paid for their tickets, appreciated the Concorde and became intensely loyal to the sleek jet. A 1978 British Airways survey showed that 43 per cent of its Concorde passengers had flown on the plane more than once. Almost half these repeaters had flown at least three times. Five had made more than 50 Concorde trips, and the record was held by the vice president of a Tennessee pencil-manufacturing firm who had made 63 supersonic crossings of the Atlantic. But even with such loyal customers, the flights between Europe and North America could not turn a profit. The Bahrain and Buenos Aires routes showed even less potential, and these would eventually be suspended when less than half the Concorde's seats were regularly filled.

To the bitter disappointment of Britain and France, the Concorde still was not selling. With the plane attracting so few new passengers, any airline that purchased it would have to battle British Airways and Air France for their customers. What the Concorde needed more than anything else was to attract a broader cross section of the flying public than it was getting. But while fares for other jet flights were decreasing, thanks to the greater carrying capacity of the 747, the cost of a Concorde ticket remained out of reach for all but a handful of travelers.

In September 1979, the British and French governments bit the bullet and agreed to halt production of the Concorde after only 16 had been completed. At a cost to them of $500 million each, it was the most expensive—and most disappointing—airliner the world had yet seen.

Since the early 1960s, the Concorde and the colossal Boeing 747 had all but monopolized conversation in commercial aviation circles. But another plane would win its share of attention.

Europeans, like Americans, were beginning to travel by air in rapidly escalating numbers. Airways on the Continent were threatened by the congestion that seemed likely to clog jet lanes in the United States. One way to alleviate such dangerous crowding would be to introduce larger jets with greater seating capacity, thus reducing the number of smaller planes flying the same routes. No matter how big the 747 might be, it was not the answer, any more than the 707 and DC-8 had been a decade earlier. All three were built for long-range service, which made them uneconomical on most short European runs.

Aware of the need for bigger planes, French and British builders, later joined by the Germans, set about in 1966 designing a wide-body airliner that could take off from short runways and fly the limited distances between European cities. The new plane, named the Airbus A300, would be built by Sud Aviation in Toulouse and powered by two Rolls-Royce or General Electric turbofan engines.

But the Europeans were slow to move the project ahead and this gave the United States a chance to get into the game. In the spring of 1966,

American Airlines' chief engineer Frank Kolk visited Lockheed in Burbank, California, to discuss a new airliner to use on the heavily traveled route between New York and Chicago. "Frank had with him," recalled William Hannon, Lockheed's chief engineer, "a little five-page typed document that he called a requirement." He wanted a fuselage, continued Hannan, "that could carry a maximum number of people at a minimum cost per seat mile. To him this meant two engines, not three or four." But most important, the aircraft had to be able to fly out of New York's La Guardia Airport, which had a strict limit of 270,000 pounds on a plane's overall weight, about 110,000 pounds heavier than a Boeing 727. Could such an aircraft be built? While Hannon pondered the question, Kolk pressed on to Long Beach and presented his "requirement" to Douglas.

Douglas and Lockheed both responded eagerly. Indeed, Lockheed had already done some work in this direction. When it lost the SST contract to Boeing, it found itself with 1,200 surplus engineers. The company assigned them to the task of designing a wide-body.

Any hopes that Douglas had of catching up with Lockheed were soon dashed. The company was in shambles. One of its oldest customers, Eastern, had sued for delayed DC-9 deliveries. The DC-8 program was in the red despite fairly good sales. DC-8 and DC-9 orders, in fact, were partly responsible for the disarray. To meet the brisk demand, especially for the DC-9, Douglas had expanded its production lines—but lacked skilled laborers to work on them. Training costs had risen as efficiency went down, and there were shortages of materials. All these factors conspired to wreck delivery schedules. Faced with a struggle to meet its payroll, Douglas accepted a merger with McDonnell Aircraft of St. Louis, a company that normally specialized in military aircraft. The transfusion of McDonnell cash saved Douglas from bankruptcy.

Lockheed was convinced that it was so far ahead of McDonnell-Douglas on the design of a wide-body that there was nothing to worry about. It had interested other airlines besides American in its plane, though a third engine would be required for takeoff from short runways. Even American agreed to the modification. The design had been refined during 10,000 hours of testing scale models in a wind tunnel. The result, by spring of 1967, was a completed design for a 300-passenger airliner, powered by Rolls-Royce engines. Called the L-1011 TriStar, the new jet looked to its creators like a sure winner. But when Lockheed paused to check on the competition, it discovered, to its surprise, that McDonnell-Douglas was gaining on it—and rapidly.

McDonnell-Douglas' plane was the DC-10. Powered by three General Electric turbofans, it closely resembled the TriStar. The only conspicuous difference between the two was the placement of the third engine. In the TriStar, as in the Boeing 727, it had been mounted behind the cabin in the fuselage. In the DC-10, it was perched above the fuselage in the middle of the tail. This position saved weight, simplified

Ground controllers: wizards of the airways

The end-all, be-all of air traffic control can be described in a single word: separation. From the moment a jetliner pulls away from the terminal at one airport until it taxis to a stop at another, it is kept a safe distance from other planes by men and women on the ground, most of whom know the flight only as a coded blip on a computerized radar screen.

After takeoff, responsibility for the airliner passes from the airport tower to a departure controller. Then, when the plane is about 30 miles away, the responsibility is assumed by the first of a succession of en-route controllers at regional centers approximately 300 miles apart. An approach controller picks up the flight as it nears its destination, and six miles from the airport, the tower takes over to monitor the landing and direct the airliner to the correct gate.

When traffic is light, each controller may be responsible for only one or two planes at any moment. But during rush hours at busy airports, the number can increase to 15. Keeping so many aircraft from colliding demands cool nerves and split-second timing. One controller, asked what kind of people are good at his work, replied: "Not the ones that take a lot of time making up their minds."

From a radar control room in Garden City, Long Island, planes are guided through the congested airspace above the New York metropolitan area's three major airports— Newark, Kennedy and La Guardia. The controller at the console in the foreground handles departures from La Guardia.

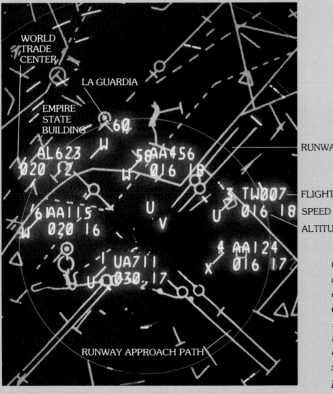

RUNWAY APPROACH PATH

FLIGHT NUMBER
SPEED
ALTITUDE

On the radar screen in the control tower at Kennedy, airliners designated by number-and-letter codes move across a map of the airport environs. American Airlines Flight 124 (AA124), flying at 1,600 feet and 170 knots, will shortly turn right to land. All but one of the other flights on the scope will soon follow it into Kennedy. The Allegheny plane (AL623) is headed for La Guardia.

maintenance and made for a more spacious cabin than in the TriStar, allowing a few more seats. American quickly became converted to the Douglas plane and, in February 1968, announced that it would buy 25 DC-10s and take options on 25 more. A month later, United Air Lines ordered 30 DC-10s and took options on another 30, thereby assuring McDonnell-Douglas of enough sales to make it feasible for the company to go ahead with the plane. Despite the unexpected competition, Lockheed had reason of its own to feel encouraged. Eastern Air Lines ordered 50 TriStars, TWA 44 and Air Holdings, Limited, a British company, another 50 to sell around the world.

The initiative originally held by Airbus Industrie, the European consortium formed to design and construct the A300, now belonged to the Americans. Airbus engineers were still tinkering with the A300's design, attempting to shrink the plane, which, with room for more than 300 passengers, was viewed as too large. The Europeans had lost an opportunity to dominate the American market. By the time the A300 made its first flight late in 1972, Lockheed's L-1011 TriStar had already

With components manufactured in five different countries, three Airbus Industrie A300 transports are assembled in the Aérospatiale factory in Toulouse, France. The wide-bodied Airbus carries the same maximum number of passengers—345— as Lockheed's TriStar L-1011, but with one less engine the European jet is more economical to operate on short-haul routes.

been in service for six months, and the DC-10 had been plying the skies for more than a year.

During that period, the DC-10 suffered a terrible setback. On June 12, 1972, an American Airlines DC-10 had just taken off from Detroit when a cargo door blew off as the jetliner was being pressurized. The sudden decompression buckled the cabin floor, rupturing some of the hydraulic control lines that ran underneath. Had the 15 rows of seats in the rear of the cabin been occupied, the additional weight might have severed all the control lines and the pilot would have been helpless. Because the seats were empty, the pilot managed to land the plane in one piece.

An investigation determined that the latch on the cargo door had been at fault. Its design was changed to make it easier to close securely, and new latches were fitted to all DC-10s—all, that is, but two. Both had come off the assembly line without the latch modifications. One of them was found and modified before an accident could occur; the other, a special high-capacity model with seats for more than 300 passengers delivered to Turkish Airlines, somehow was not.

On March 3, 1973, the Turkish plane, carrying 116 passengers from Istanbul, landed in Paris. From there, it took off for London with more than 200 additional passengers who had been stranded in Paris by an

At the Lockheed plant in Palmdale, California, workers ready the 19-foot-wide passenger cabin of a TriStar L-1011 for final outfitting. Seen in the background are two shafts for elevators that will carry flight attendants to and from the galley below.

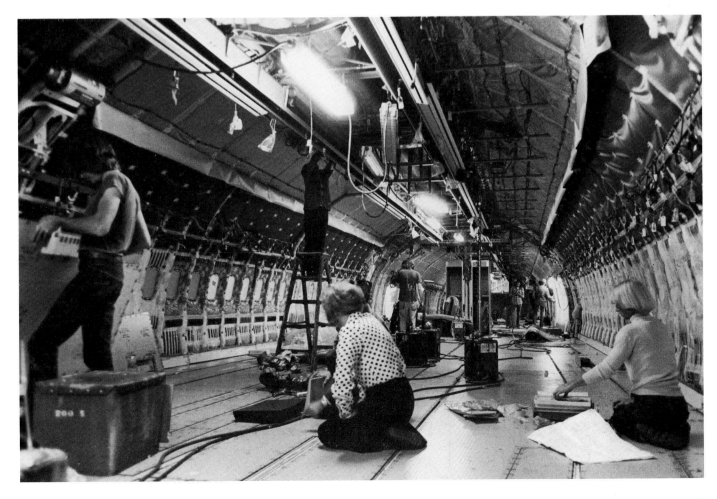

airline strike in Britain that had forced the cancellation of a BEA flight. Over France, the latch, improperly fastened before takeoff, gave way. The weight of a full load of passengers caused the cabin floor to collapse completely, and the plane plunged to earth, killing all 346 aboard.

There were no other incidents for more than six years. Then on May 25, 1979, as an American Airlines DC-10 left Chicago bound for Los Angeles, the left engine tore off. The plane continued to climb to about 300 feet and then rolled to the left until the wings were almost vertical. All lift was lost and the airplane fell out of the sky. By the time the DC-10 crashed, it had turned almost completely over. Again there were no survivors.

After the accident, all DC-10s were grounded pending an investigation, which disclosed that a maintenance crew had cracked the engine mount while removing the turbofan for maintenance. Though it had been exonerated, the DC-10 became the target of much criticism and concern. The pilots never lost faith in the plane, but for months afterward, many people refused to fly on it.

After an initial rush of orders, sales of both the DC-10 and the Tri-Star slowed down dramatically. Douglas had found customers for nearly 300 DC-10s. Lockheed sold 244 TriStars, a large number but not enough to recover development costs and losses incurred during years when sales were slow. All told, Lockheed would lose an estimated $2.5 billion on the plane.

In Europe the Airbus A300, first flown on October 28, 1972, was just hitting its stride. Fitted with only two engines and with innovative, lightweight wings, it was proving to be inexpensive to operate. Air France had put the first A300 into service in May 1974, and in the months that followed, the airliner sold briskly in Europe and Asia. Korean Air Lines and Thai Airways International each purchased several of the craft in 1975. Lufthansa, Indian Air Lines and South African Airways were among others that agreed to buy the A300.

With the virtues of the Airbus now well known, American carriers began taking an active interest in the plane. Eastern had been looking for a two-engined aircraft with the latest technology in turbofans and airframe to fly nonstop between New York and Miami. The Airbus fit the bill, except for one thing—it contained more seats than Eastern thought it could fill.

Eastern officials prepared to negotiate with Airbus Industrie. One of the chief Airbus salesmen was George Warde, a jovial horse trader who had once been president of American Airlines and now headed the European consortium's North American operations. The other was Airbus vice president Roger Beteille. Eastern badly needed replacement aircraft for its aging 727 fleet, and Airbus Industrie badly needed a foothold in the U.S. market.

When the bargaining began, Eastern's president Frank Borman, the former astronaut, asked bluntly, "Why should we buy your airplane?"

"Because if you don't you're dead," Warde replied. He knew that

Incorporating the latest advances in electronics, the flight deck of a Boeing 767 glows with information being fed from computers aboard the aircraft to small television screens on the instrument panel. The computers not only help the pilot fly the new airliner, but also diagnose malfunctions to help mechanics with maintenance.

fuel and maintenance costs on Eastern's aging 727s were shrinking the airline's profits.

When Borman brought up his concern about filling most of the Airbus' seats, Beteille made an unprecedented move. He offered to reduce the price of the A300; once Eastern's traffic grew to a point where the seats were being filled, the airline could pay the difference between the original asking price and the reduced one. Warde called this arrangement "operating support." Borman, after conferring with his vice president for finance, Charles Simons, tentatively agreed to the proposal on the condition that Eastern be allowed to borrow four A300s and fly passengers in them for six months before the contract was signed. Beteille's initial reaction was shock; Eastern might as well have asked that the Eiffel Tower be moved to Miami Beach. But Simons argued convincingly that the four planes would be "four flying advertisements." Though Beteille still remained dubious, Warde was convinced that a six-month trial would clinch the deal. Even before the six months were over, Borman knew the A300 was a superb airplane; it drew raves from pilots. On April 6, 1978, Eastern signed for 23 aircraft at $25 million apiece.

Borman was roundly criticized as unpatriotic for buying a foreign airplane. He retorted that more than a third of the A300's price went for components made in America, particularly its General Electric engines. Besides, the deal was irresistible. No airline had ever been given more favorable terms in a new-plane contract.

Eastern's publicly and privately expressed satisfaction with the A300 was the testimonial that the plane needed. Before Airbus Industrie signed with Eastern, it had not sold an A300 in a year and a half. Though there was no rush to the Airbus by other U.S. airlines, during 1979 the company supplied 38 per cent of the wide-body jets purchased by non-Communist countries.

Ever since 1958 and the smashing success of the Boeing 707, the Americans had practically owned the skies. But the A300 changed that. The plane found a secure niche for itself and filled it before American aircraft manufacturers could respond with a twin-engined wide-body that matched the A300's economy. Only Boeing had plans for one, its 767. McDonnell-Douglas and Lockheed, after toying with variations of aircraft that were already in service, elected to abandon the field to the Airbus.

Though Eastern used the A300 successfully to replace an aging fleet of 727s, the plane was too big and too expensive for most airlines to use for that purpose. Boeing recognized that the 727 had seen better days and had another new plane—the 757, a jetliner with the same diameter as a 727—on the drawing board to replace it. Incorporating the most up-to-date engine and airframe technology, the 757 promised lower fuel consumption, less noise and cleaner exhaust than the 727. But it was expensive, too, and airlines faced with cutthroat competition and a severe economic recession that stiffened customer resistance to the higher fares that might help defray the cost of the new plane, were more reluctant than ever to sign up for new planes.

Whatever the future may hold for airlines and plane builders, the jetliner has already left an indelible mark. Jets carry 300 million passengers annually in the United States alone and fly 97 per cent of their scheduled flights, often in weather that would have grounded airliners a short 25 years ago. Even so, the safety record of jets, despite well-publicized accidents, far surpasses that of piston aircraft. Jets account for more than 90 per cent of all U.S. intercity travel in public transportation. In 1960, when the jet age was less than two years old, only 10 per cent of Americans older than 18 had ever flown in a scheduled airliner; by the early 1980s the figure had risen to 65 per cent. In two and a half decades, jets have made air travel a common fact of life—accepted, trusted, routine. ➤➤

Three Boeing 767s (foreground) head a line-up of 737s, 727s and an Air Force E-3 radar reconnaissance plane at the company's South Seattle, Washington, plant. The 767s are part of a fleet of five test aircraft undergoing trials to certify the new wide-body for airline service.

The day of the jumbo jets

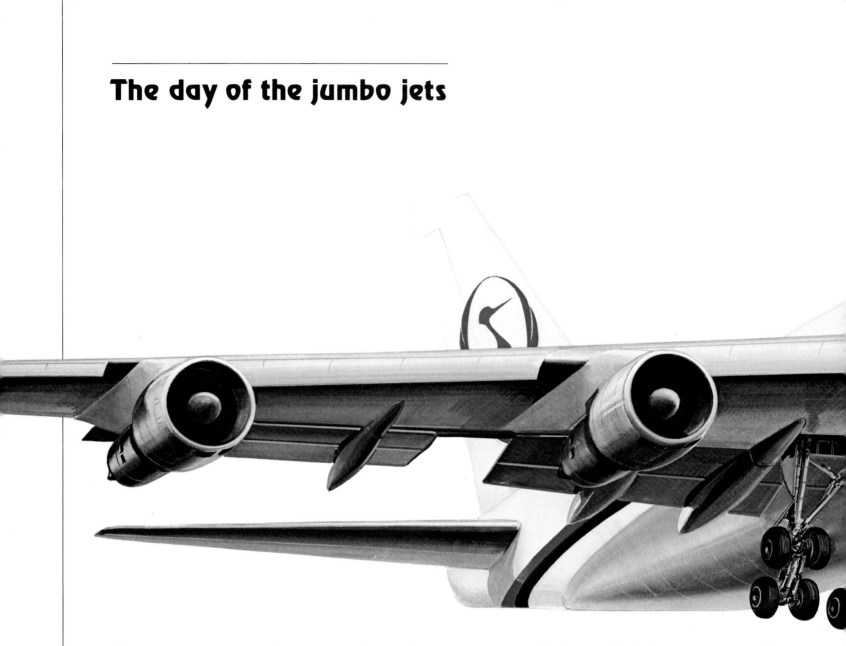

"I took one look," recalled San Francisco homemaker Ginny Clausen, "and I said to myself, 'Oh, nothing this big is going to fly.'" That was a typical response in the early 1970s to the new Boeing 747, the world's first jumbo jet airliner and the forerunner of all the wide-bodied jet transports shown here and on the following pages. This type of jetliner soon caught on, however, and the number of people traveling by jet increased dramatically. By 1974 some 45 million more Americans had flown than was the case only six years earlier, a 28 per cent increase that would have been unthinkable before the wide-body revolution.

Embodying the latest technology, each of the big planes was designed to carry large numbers of passengers varying distances—from flights of 6,000 miles to some of no more than 100 miles. The four-engined 747, with its 499-seat capacity, was built primarily for long-range routes. Inspired by its example, European manufacturers pioneered the short-haul wide-body with their twin-engined 281-passenger Airbus A300. But the American plane makers Douglas and Lockheed beat them to the intermediate-range marketplace with their DC-10 and L-1011 respectively, both high-density trijets that could carry approximately 350 passengers. The more recent twin-engined Boeing 767, which appeared in 1982, represents America's attempt to capture the twin-engined wide-body market of the 1980s and beyond. Designed to operate with maximum efficiency in the face of rising fuel costs, it extends what one writer called the "spacious age" of twin-aisle passenger cabin comfort to routes never before served by wide-body airliners.

BOEING 747-100 (1970)
The Boeing 747 has a massive 18-wheel undercarriage—shown here lowered in touchdown position—to cushion landings and distribute the plane's 390-ton weight evenly on the runway. The 747 cruises at 580 mph and has a range of 7,090 miles.

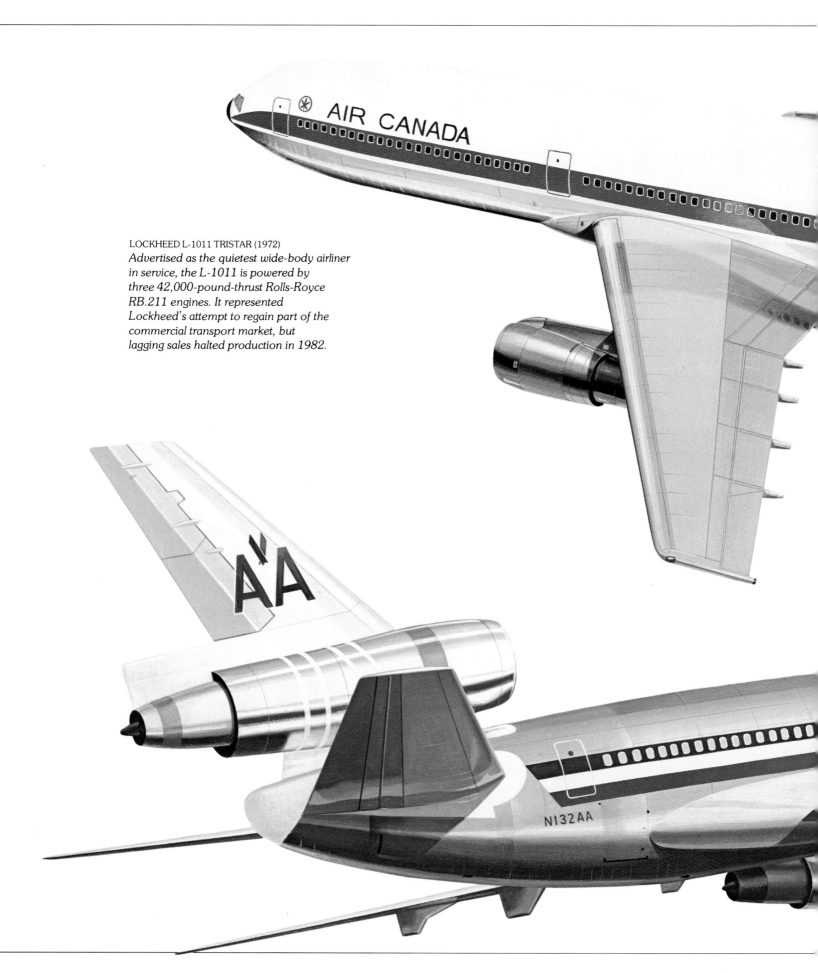

LOCKHEED L-1011 TRISTAR (1972)
Advertised as the quietest wide-body airliner in service, the L-1011 is powered by three 42,000-pound-thrust Rolls-Royce RB.211 engines. It represented Lockheed's attempt to regain part of the commercial transport market, but lagging sales halted production in 1982.

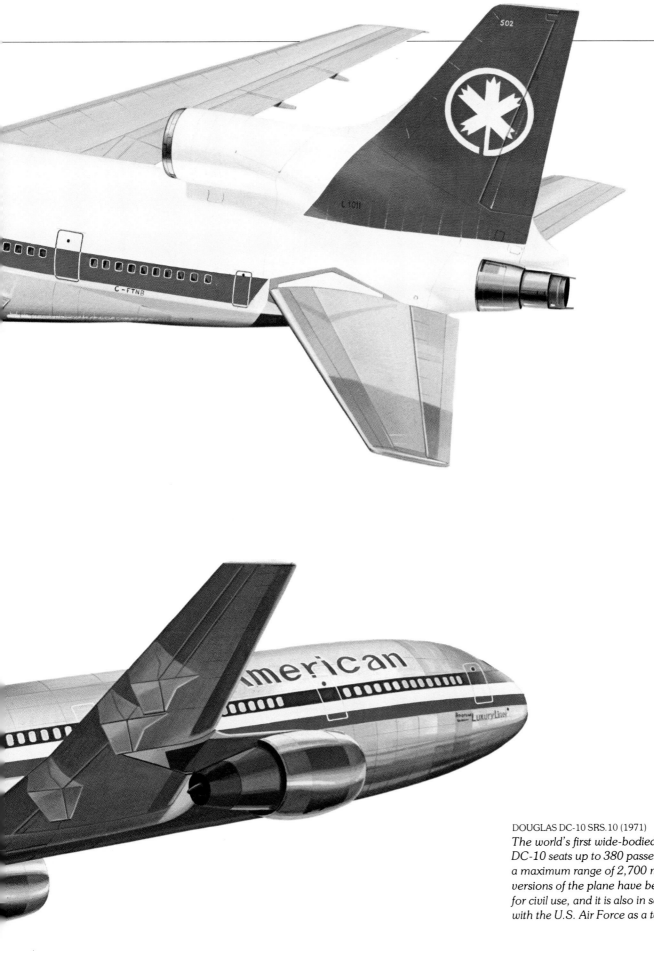

DOUGLAS DC-10 SRS.10 (1971)
The world's first wide-bodied trijet, the DC-10 seats up to 380 passengers and has a maximum range of 2,700 miles. Many versions of the plane have been produced for civil use, and it is also in service with the U.S. Air Force as a tanker.

BOEING 767-200 (1983)
Representing yet another gamble on the future by Boeing, the 767 uses an advanced wing structure and weight-saving composite materials to compete economically over such routes as San Francisco-Cleveland, Los Angeles-Miami and London-Cairo. It seats up to 289 passengers.

SX-BEB

UNITED

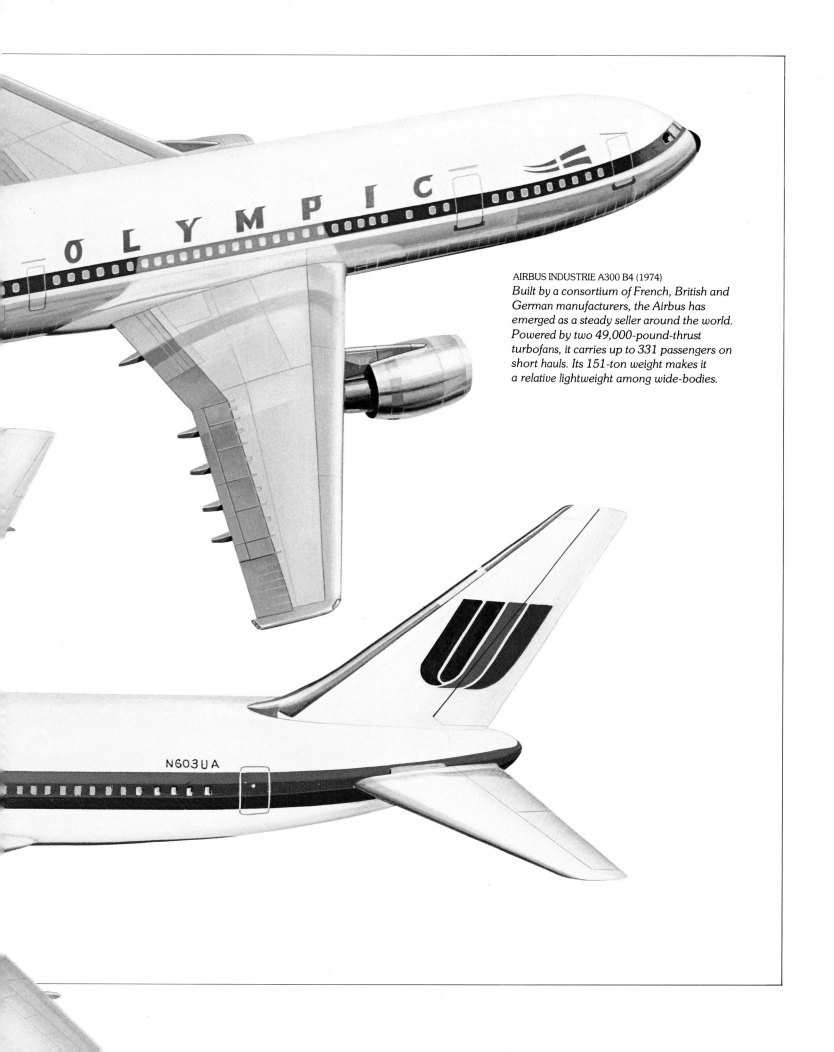

AIRBUS INDUSTRIE A300 B4 (1974)
Built by a consortium of French, British and German manufacturers, the Airbus has emerged as a steady seller around the world. Powered by two 49,000-pound-thrust turbofans, it carries up to 331 passengers on short hauls. Its 151-ton weight makes it a relative lightweight among wide-bodies.

A jetport for today—and tomorrow

When the commercial jet age dawned in the 1950s, airports rushed to enlarge and modernize existing facilities, trying to keep pace with the progress of planes and the great increase in travelers. Then the jumbo jets arrived, and the resulting confusion on the ground was, in the words of one American aviation official, "like the Queen Mary docking every 30 minutes." Airports of completely new design were clearly needed.

Fortunately, the problems had been anticipated by far-sighted airport planners from Frankfurt, Germany, to Dallas-Fort Worth in Texas. Among these were the architects and engineers of the Paris Airport Authority, who in 1966 began to build an extraordinary jetport on 7,670 acres 16 miles northeast of the French capital.

Aéroport Charles de Gaulle was neither the biggest nor the busiest jetport in the world when it opened in 1974, but it could lay claim to being the most futuristic. The airport was designed to meet Paris air traffic needs well into the 21st Century; plans call for it to grow to as many as nine passenger terminals.

The first of these terminals, Aérogare 1—seen on the following pages in photographs taken around the time of its inauguration—is a tour de force of stark, efficient design. At the center of its operations is a doughnut-shaped concrete structure about the size of Rome's Colosseum— 660 feet in diameter and 100 feet high. Its top three levels, reached by ramps, provide parking space for close to 4,000 cars; the next three levels are used for passenger handling; the lower levels house shops, restaurants and facilities for baggage sorting. And in the middle of the doughnut is what the designers called the "central void."

Crisscrossing this well are six surrealistic transparent tubes fitted with conveyor belts that whisk some 10 million people a year from level to level of the three passenger-processing floors of the terminal. Seven tunnels—each approximately 550 feet long and equipped with moving sidewalks—link the main Aérogare 1 building to seven satellite terminals where more than 100,000 planes a year are loaded, unloaded and serviced.

A series of obliquely angled turnoffs from a runway (far right) at Aéroport Charles de Gaulle throws a pattern of jet-age whorls across the French countryside. These high-speed turnoffs enable jets to clear the airport's two 11,880-foot runways without slowing down to make a 90-degree turn.

The 262-foot control tower—which appears to lean in this picture because of camera-lens parallax—contains radar apparatus, radios and computers. Additional equipment is housed in the navigation center below the tower.

Through softly lit tunnels between the satellite terminals and the main building of the jetport, travelers glide along moving sidewalks, passing beneath advertisements beamed onto overhead globes.

Seven satellite terminals—each capable of handling four wide-body jets at a time—ring Aérogare 1's main terminal. They were given a triangular shape so that planes could easily maneuver into and out of the docking areas and still be close to the terminal.

Passengers glide through an inclined tube connected with the transfer level of the main terminal. Such tubes separate arriving and departing passengers, decreasing the distances they would otherwise have to walk.

In this fisheye-lens view taken from a helicopter, six conveyor tubes swoop from level to level in the 11-story Aérogare 1, high above its central illuminated fountain.

A bilingual information board hangs above one of the terminal's modernistic sofas. Another sofa remains covered in this picture taken before the airport's opening.

One of 32 booths designed for drive-up ticketing and baggage checking sits empty outside the terminal. Too costly to equip and run, the booths were never used.

After luggage has been checked inside the terminal and sorted by hand, unmanned, computer-controlled tractors following buried electronic guidance cables tow baggage carts to the planes.

A flexible motorized loading bridge extends from a satellite terminal to an Air France Concorde, ready for boarding for the first supersonic passenger flight to Rio de Janeiro, on January 21, 1976.

In the eerie predawn glow of fluorescent lights around its rim and along the approaching roads, Aérogare 1 waits for a new day's passengers.

Acknowledgments

The index for this book was prepared by Gale Linck Partoyan. For their valuable help in the preparation of this volume, the editors wish to thank: **In France:** Paris—René Farion, Air France; Colonel Edmond Petit, Musée Air-France; Jacques Reder, Aéroports de Paris; Général Pierre Lissarague, Director, Colonel Pierre Willefert, Curator, Musée de l'Air; Suresnes—Jean-Claude Caillou, Aérospatiale; Vincennes—Marcellin Hodeir, S.H.A.A. **In Great Britain:** Bristol—Howard Berry, British Aerospace; Bury St. Edmunds—A. D. D. Henshaw; Farnborough—D. W. Goode, Royal Aircraft Establishment; Hatfield—John Scott, Darrell Cott, British Aerospace; Hendon—R. W. Mack, P. Merton, M. Tagg, Royal Air Force Museum; London—A. Gibson; Sir Arnold Hall; T. Charman, E. Hines, J. S. Lucas, J. W. Pavey, M. J. Willis, Imperial War Museum; John Bagley, Martin Andrewartha, Science Museum; Oldbury—M. Daunt; Weybridge—Norman Barfield, British Aerospace. **In Italy:** Rome—Countess Maria Fede Caproni, Museo Aeronautico Caproni di Taliedo. **In the United States:** Arizona—John Meyer, Pam Pennegar, Gates Learjet; California—Harry Gann, Douglas Aircraft Company; Emerald Jones, Sol London, Rich Stadler, Lockheed-California Company; Connecticut—Jim Devaney, Harvey Lippincott, Robert Weiss, United Technologies' Pratt & Whitney; Washington, D.C.—Fred Farrer, Mike Harris, Edmund P. Kennedy, Donald Shaklee, Federal Aviation Administration; Philip Edwards, Donald Lopez, Pete Suthard, Robert van der Linden, National Air and Space Museum; James Waters, United Airlines; Georgia—Everett Hayes, Dick Martin, Lockheed-Georgia Company; Maryland—Adele C. Schwartz, *Airport Forum;* Missouri—Gordon Le Bert, McDonnell-Douglas Corporation; New York—Berl Brechner, *Flying* magazine; Ann Whyte, Pan American World Airways; Pennsylvania—James F. Krick; Texas—Al Becker, American Airlines; Barbara Potter, Braniff International Airlines; Washington—Floyd Baldwin, Bruce A. Berkbigler, Lonna Brooks, Tom Cole, Leslie R. Harcus, Marilyn Phipps, Paul Spitzer, Gordon Williams, Boeing Commercial Airplane Company. **In West Germany:** Bonn—General Adolf Galland (Ret.); Mainz-Finthen—Karl Ries; Munich—Hans Ebert, Messerschmitt-Bölkow-Blohm.

Bibliography

Allen, Roy, *Major Airports of the World.* Shepperton, England: Ian Allen, 1979.

Beaty, David, *The Water Jump: The Story of Transatlantic Flight.* Harper & Row, 1976.

Blackall, T. E., *Concorde: The story, the facts and the figures.* Henley-on-Thames, England: G. T. Foulis, 1969.

Bowers, Peter M., *Boeing Aircraft since 1916.* Aero, 1966.

Boyne, Walter J., and Donald S. Lopez, *The Jet Age: Forty Years of Jet Aviation.* National Air and Space Museum, Smithsonian Institution, 1979.

Bright, Charles D., *The Jet Makers: The Aerospace Industry from 1945 to 1972.* The Regents Press of Kansas, 1978.

Calvert, Brian, *Flying Concorde.* St. Martin's Press, 1982.

Christy, Joe, *The Learjet.* Tab Books, 1979.

Costello, John, and Terry Hughes, *The Concorde Conspiracy.* Scribner's, 1976.

Cunningham, Frank, *Sky Master: The Story of Donald Douglas.* Dorrance and Company, 1943.

Daley, Robert, *An American Saga: Juan Trippe and His Pan Am Empire.* Random House, 1980.

Davies, R. E. G., *Airlines of the United States since 1914.* London: Putnam, 1972.

Eddy, Paul, Elaine Potter and Bruce Page, *Destination Disaster: From the Tri-Motor to the DC-10: The Risk of Flying.* Quandrangle/The New York Times Book Co., 1976.

Encyclopedia of Aviation. Scribner's, 1977.

Godson, John, *Runway.* Scribner's, 1973.

Green, William, and Gordon Swanborough, *The Illustrated Encyclopedia of the World's Commercial Aircraft.* London: Salamander Books, 1978.

Greif, Martin, *The Airport Book: From Landing Field to Modern Terminal.* Mayflower, 1979.

Halaby, Najeeb E., *Crosswinds: An Airman's Memoir.* Doubleday, 1978.

Heiman, Grover, *Jet Pioneers.* Duell, Sloan and Pearce, 1963.

Herron, Edward A., *Cobra in the Sky: The Supersonic Transport.* Macmillan, 1968.

Hooftman, Hugo, *Russian Aircraft.* Aero, 1965.

Hopkins, George E., *The Airline Pilots, A Study in Elite Unionization.* Harvard University Press, 1971.

Hubler, Richard G., *Big Eight: A Biography of an Airplane.* Duell, Sloan and Pearce, 1960.

Ingells, Douglas J.:
L-1011 TriStar and the Lockheed Story. Aero, 1973.
The McDonnell Douglas Story. Aero, 1979.
747: Story of the Boeing Super Jet. Aero, 1970.

Jackson, A. J., *British Civil Aircraft since 1919, Vol. 3.* London: Putnam, 1960.

Kuter, Laurence S., *The Great Gamble: The Boeing 747.* University of Alabama Press, 1973.

McClement, Fred, *It Doesn't Matter Where You Sit.* Holt, Rinehart and Winston, 1969.

Mansfield, Harold, *Vision: The Story of Boeing.* Duell, Sloan and Pearce, 1966.

Miller, Ronald, and David Sawers, *The Technical Development of Modern Aviation.* Praeger Publishers, 1970.

Nayler, J. L., *Aviation: its technical development.* London: Peter Owen/Vision Press, 1965.

Pudney, John, *The Seven Skies: A Study of B.O.A.C. and its Forerunners since 1919.* London: Putnam, 1959.

Rickenbacker, Edward V., *Rickenbacker.* Prentice-Hall, 1967.

Schiff, Barry J., *The Boeing 707.* Arco, 1967.

Serling, Robert J.:
From the Captain to the Colonel: An Informal History of Eastern Airlines. Dial Press, 1980.
Little Giant: The Story of Gates Learjet. Robert J. Serling, 1974.
Loud and Clear. Doubleday, 1969.
The Only Way to Fly. Doubleday, 1976.

Sprigg, C. St. John, *British Airways.* London: Thomas Nelson and Sons, 1934.

Taylor, Frank J., *High Horizons: The United Airlines Story.* McGraw-Hill, 1964.

Taylor, John W. R., ed., *Jane's Pocket Book of Commercial Transport Aircraft.* Macmillan, 1974.

Taylor, Richard L., *Instrument Flying.* Macmillan, 1978.

Varley, Helen, ed., *The Air Traveler's Handbook.* Simon and Schuster, 1978.

Whitehouse, Arch, *The Sky's the Limit: A History of the U. S. Airlines.* Macmillan, 1971.

Picture credits

The sources for the illustrations in this book are listed below. Credits from left to right are separated by semicolons, from top to bottom by dashes. Endpaper (and cover detail, regular edition): Painting by Frank Wootton. 6, 7: Courtesy McDonnell-Douglas Corporation. 8, 9: Courtesy McDonnell-Douglas Corporation; courtesy Pan American World Airways—Courtesy McDonnell-Douglas Corporation. 10, 11: Courtesy Boeing Commercial Airplane Company, except upper right, courtesy Pan American World Airways (2). 12, 13: Courtesy Lockheed-California Company (2); Peter Stackpole for *Life*. 14, 15: Leon Dishman, courtesy National Air and Space Museum, Smithsonian Institution—The Bettmann Archive; Musée Air-France, Paris (2). 16, 17: Collection of Richard Smith—Allan Grant for *Life*; Royal Air Force Museum, Hendon. 18, 19: Cornell Capa for *Life*. 20: Fox Photos, Ltd., London. 23: Diagrams by Another Color, Inc. 25: Leon Dishman, courtesy National Air and Space Museum, Smithsonian Institution. 26: Tass, Moscow—Leon Dishman, courtesy National Air and Space Museum, Smithsonian Institution. 27: Reg Corlett, courtesy de Havilland Aircraft of Canada, Ltd.—Terry Shwetz, courtesy de Havilland Aircraft of Canada, Ltd. 29-31: Courtesy British Aerospace, Hatfield. 32, 33: de Havilland Aircraft Co., Ltd., courtesy Ron Davies Collection. 34: Courtesy British Aerospace, Hatfield. 35: Central Press Photos, Ltd., London. 36, 37: Drawing by John Batchelor. 38: Jim Burke for *Life*. 39-45: Popperfoto, London. 46: Imperial War Museum, London (2)—Popperfoto, London. 47: Associated Press, London. 48, 49: Royal Aircraft Establishment, Farnborough, Crown Copyright Reserved. 50: UPI. 51: Popperfoto, London. 52, 53: Royal Aircraft Establishment, Farnborough, Crown Copyright Reserved. 54-57: Courtesy Boeing Commercial Airplane Company. 59: Courtesy British Aerospace, Weybridge. 60, 61: Courtesy Boeing Commercial Airplane Company. 62, 63: Drawing by John Batchelor. 64: Howard Sochurek for *Life*—Sovfoto. 65: Sovfoto. 67: George Silk for *Life*. 68: Burt Glinn from Magnum Photos. 69: George Silk for *Life*. 70, 71: Courtesy McDonnell-Douglas Corporation. 72-79: Courtesy Boeing Commercial Airplane Company. 80, 81: Leon Dishman, courtesy National Air and Space Museum, Smithsonian Institution. 82: Courtesy Boeing Commercial Airplane Company. 84: Wide World. 85: Frank Scherschel for *Life*. 86, 87: Drawing by John Batchelor. 88, 89: Ernest Barter, courtesy James F. Krick. 90, 91: Bob Bryant for the *San Francisco Examiner*; James F. Krick. 92, 93: N. R. Farbman; Fran Oritz for the *San Francisco Examiner*. 95: Éditions Cercle d'Art, Paris—courtesy Braniff International. 96: John Sadovy. 98, 99: Diagrams by Another Color, Inc. 101: Drawing by John Huehnergarth for *Life*. 102: © 1979 Herman J. Kokojan from Black Star. 104: Musée Air France, Paris. 105: Courtesy British Aerospace, Hatfield. 106, 109: Courtesy Boeing Commercial Airplane Company. 110: Courtesy Boeing Commercial Airplane Company—diagrams by Another Color, Inc. 113: Gordon Tenney—courtesy Gates Learjet Corporation—© Jim Sugar from Black Star. 115: Courtesy McDonnell-Douglas Corporation. 117: Courtesy Boeing Commercial Airplane Company. 118-123: Drawings by John Batchelor. 124, 125: Courtesy British Aerospace, Bristol. 131: Tass from Sovfoto; James H. Pickerell for *Aviation Week and Space Technology* © by McGraw-Hill, Inc. (5) 132: Diagrams by Another Color, Inc. 134-140: Courtesy Boeing Commercial Airplane Company. 142: © Yan from Rapho/Photo Researchers. 143: Arthur Gibson, London. 144, 145: Drawings by John Batchelor. 146: Courtesy British Aerospace, Bristol. 149: Enrico Ferorelli from Wheeler Pictures. 150: James Andanson from Sygma. 151: Diego Goldberg from Sygma. 153-155: Courtesy Boeing Commercial Airplane Company. 156-161: Drawings by John Batchelor. 162, 163: Alain Nogues from Sygma. 164, 165: Georges Beutter from Gamma/Liaison; Jean Gaumy from Gamma/Liaison—Georges Beutter from Gamma/Liaison. 166, 167: © Phelps from Rapho/Photo Researchers—Georges Beutter from Gamma/Liaison; Alain Nogues from Sygma. 168, 169: Georges Beutter from Gamma/Liaison (2)—Jean Gaumy from Gamma/Liaison. 170, 171: Frederic Proust from Sygma.